REFLECTIONS OF A LONE TRAVELLER

REFLECTIONS OF A LONE TRAVELLER

The Tale of One Man's Journey across the World and His Encounters with People and Places

MADHAVAN KAVANAL

Notion Press

Old No. 38, New No. 6
McNichols Road, Chetpet
Chennai - 600 031

First Published by Notion Press 2016
Copyright © Madhavan Kavanal 2016
All Rights Reserved.

ISBN 978-1-945926-54-9

This book has been published with all efforts taken to make the material error-free after the consent of the author. However, the author and the publisher do not assume and hereby disclaim any liability to any party for any loss, damage, or disruption caused by errors or omissions, whether such errors or omissions result from negligence, accident, or any other cause.

No part of this book may be used, reproduced in any manner whatsoever without written permission from the author, except in the case of brief quotations embodied in critical articles and reviews.

Dedication

Dedicated to all the people, mainly Non-Resident Indians

CONTENTS

1. Memory of a Train Journey — 1
2. Beginnings — 8
3. The Kuwait Days — 14
4. Back Home — 22
5. Back to Work — 24
6. Buying a Coffee Estate — 33
7. A Change of Job — 38
8. The Times with the Financial Group — 49
9. Business in Mumbai — 56
10. The Granite Business — 64
11. Srinivas Goes Back to Kuwait — 70
12. Business Encounter Again in India — 80
13. On the Personal Front — 85
14. The Tale of Richard's Family — 91
15. Srinivas in the North East — 97
16. A Fresh Hope — 106

Epilogue — *119*

MEMORY OF A TRAIN JOURNEY

Srinivas boarded the Eurotrain at Milano bound for Paris. The train was speeding along the side of the Alps. The clouds had disappeared, leaving the mountainside bathed in a stream of golden European summer sunlight. The other side was a jungle of high-rise buildings. Evening was giving way to twilight and the environment was calm and serene. Srinivas thought about all he had done these past few days in Europe, everything he had done since he'd left his residence in Kuwait.

It was at the suggestion of Abu Ali, his business partner, that Srinivas had accompanied him to Damascus in Syria. One of his wife's relatives was the director of the country's petroleum refineries, and one of the refineries in Homs had been destroyed by recent Israeli bombings. They were in the process of rebuilding the complex and the director wanted some trust-worthy business house to discuss the matter with, especially to safeguard the interests of the team involved – a general practice in those parts of the world in those days – the 1970s.

Since the drawings and all related documents had been destroyed in the fire, Srinivas, with a couple of senior engineers and managers, was assigned the task of inspecting the plant, writing down the specifications of the equipment from tags and other available sources, prepare a list of the major equipment, shop for these in different countries and obtain proposals from at least three suppliers. In consultation with Abu Ali and Srinivas, the director and his team shortlisted a few potential suppliers for these items.

Since the communication network, electricity lines and other such infrastructure had been totally destroyed and though partially reinstated by that time were still erratic, it was decided that someone would have to go to these suppliers personally, discuss the urgency of the situation and collect the proposals. This task was assigned to Abu Ali's office. And Srinivas, in his capacity as its managing partner, was entrusted with the job.

His first destination was Italy. He met the concerned companies, all of whom agreed to provide the proposals in line with the requirements, and to supply the necessary equipment at the shortest time possible. His next destination was France, which would be followed first by Germany and then Belgium. The negotiations in Italy went well and Srinivas was wondering how the forthcoming meetings would be.

"Passport please!" a coarse, heavy voice – enough to startle *anybody* if heard unexpectedly– jolted Srinivas from his thoughts. He looked around. It was dark outside now. The train must have crossed the border of Italy and passed into Austria because it was Austrian immigration officers who were around, checking the passengers' travel documents. Srinivas handed over his passport and ticket. The officer went through the passport, looked at him, and then went over to his colleague who was at the other end of the compartment. They spoke to each other in German for a few minutes. The officer then came back to Srinivas and asked him; "Where are you going, Sir?"

"Paris," Srinivas replied. "I have a French visa."

"But now you are in Austria and you don't have a visa for Austria," the officer said.

Srinivas protested; "But I am just passing through Austria! I have no intention of getting down anywhere in this country!"

"No Sir. Now the train is in Austria. Even if you're just passing through this country, you need a visa. You need to get down at the next station and come with me." And with that, the officer sat down in the opposite seat. This, of course, was in the days prior to the formation of the European Union and the introduction of the Schengen Visa.

The officer led Srinivas to the immigration office at the next station. He first went inside, came back a few minutes later, and then led Srinivas to a waiting room and said; "Wait here. Head not here. Will come soon."

It was a comfortable room, but Srinivas was scared. Entering a country without a visa was a serious offence. He feared they might put him in prison, or fine him. After an hour or so, the officer returned and asked Srinivas to follow him. The head of immigration there had arrived. He signaled for Srinivas to sit opposite to him and asked some questions – what was the purpose of his visit to these countries, why had he not taken an Austrian visa and so on. Srinivas confessed that he had never thought he would need an Austrian visa since he was only passing though the country. The officers conferred among themselves for a few minutes. Then the officer asked Srinivas to follow him. They went to his office.

"Sit down," the officer said, pointing to a chair. He said then to Srinivas; "Sir, now you are in my country. You cannot enter this country without a visa. So I am giving you a visa valid for two weeks."

He stamped the visa on Srinivas' passport and handed it back saying; "Welcome to Austria, Sir. If you want to catch another train to carry on with your journey, there is one in another forty five minutes from now."

He and Srinivas then shook hands and bid each other goodbye. While these heavily-built, coarse-voiced officials appeared rude at first, Srinivas found that they were actually polite, friendly and serious people. He remembered that the land he was in was the birthplace of legends like Mozart, Beethoven, Shubert, John Strauss…and Adolf Hitler. Since he had a visa now, he was even tempted to stay and visit the historical sites. But then he remembered he had work to do and that he had to leave.

While waiting for his train, Srinivas was engrossed in his own thoughts. He remembered another funny incident which, perhaps, might only be fascinating to those who have encountered a more or less similar situation. Most Indians, when planning a trip to Europe, would not consider the journey complete without visiting London. Srinivas too felt the same way. When he had got the chance to go on his first European trip, the first place he'd gone to was London. He landed in Heathrow Airport and was filled with excitement. There were different immigration counters and one of them was marked "Commonwealth Citizens." Since India was a

Commonwealth member, he went to that counter thinking that it might offer some privileges. The officer there was an Indian-origin British –which thrilled Srinivas all the more. He handed over his passport. The officer asked for his ticket and said; "How long are you going to be here?"

"Three or four days," Srinivas replied.

"Where are you going to stay?"

"Hotel," Srinivas said. He gave the name of the hotel where he had a reservation. "And I have several business contacts here."

"What guarantee do we have that you will not take up a job here?"

Srinivas was starting to get a little annoyed. "Well, I have a respectable job in a tax-free country which is also one of the richest in the world. And I am a partner at the company I work for. So why should I want a job here?"

"Do you have enough money for your stay here?"

"Yes."

"Show me"

Srinivas took out a wad of different currencies of different denominations and showed the officer.

"Count it," he said

Srinivas lost his temper. In a loud, harsh voice he said; "Officer, enough is enough. Give me my passport back. I don't want to come into your country. I am taking the next flight to Brussels. I have a valid visa, issued by your embassy, and I have business contacts here who are expecting me.

In case my company or our partner here sustains any loss because of this, you will be responsible. I will take it up with your embassy in Kuwait." He started picking up his luggage.

Suddenly, another British immigration officer, a senior one by the look of him, appeared. He might have simply been observing the conversation between Srinivas and the officer at first, and then decided to step in when he thought things were getting out of hand.

He took the passport and looked at Srinivas. "Do you know English?"

"I am an Indian," Srinivas exploded.

"I can see that from your passport," the officer said.

"I know English well enough to know the English!" Srinivas snapped.

"What exactly is the problem?" asked the officer.

"Ask your colleague," retorted Srinivas.

The senior officer went through Srinivas' passport, his return ticket, his hotel bookings, and then turned to his colleague. "Well, he has a valid visa and all the relevant documents." He stamped Srinivas' passport, smiled and said; "Welcome to the United Kingdom Sir. Have a nice stay."

Srinivas walked away, pushing the trolley, without even saying thanks.

Srinivas later came to know that some young immigration officials harassed Asian visitors with a volley of rude questions even if they had all the valid travel documents. He heard that a central government minister of India had once been asked by a young officer for a guarantee that he would not take up employment in the UK – an event that had created some diplomatic furor between the two countries. The officer had to apologize later. Now the attitudes of the British have changed considerably and perhaps it would reflect in the immigration desks as well…

Srinivas was roused from his thoughts as his train pulled into the station. He quickly boarded and went to his seat. He still had enough time for a good sleep. He was tired, the sleeper-berth was quite comfortable and, in just a few minutes, Srinivas bid goodbye to Austria and fell into a deep slumber.

BEGINNINGS

The childhood of Srinivas was not easy. His was an aristocratic family with a fine past to boast of, but hardly earned enough to make ends meet given that it was a family with seven growing children. The income came from some small ancestral properties which provided rice, pepper, coconuts and so on, along with the salary of Srinivas' father who was the headmaster of a government school. But the family was keen that the children get a good education at all costs. As the children grew, the expenses increased accordingly. One child was in college, three were in secondary and higher secondary classes and the rest were in primary school. But, as the expenses mounted, there was no increase in income. This led to borrowing from close relatives, sometimes to pay the school or college fees or examination fees on time. Often, the relatives would harass them if they didn't repay on time, even though the amounts borrowed were small.

Srinivas realized very early on that unless the family income was enhanced, there were going to be problems. Relief came when his eldest brother got a government job upon completing his graduation. He had passed a competitive examination while in his final year of college. In the 1950s, in the rural areas of the country, graduating and getting a government job was considered quite prestigious. The additional income definitely helped, but Srinivas and one of his younger siblings were in college and, given this increase in expenses, even the increased income was not enough. And so Srinivas decided to quit college and look for a job. He was in his final year at this time. He remembered that he had a relative who was a manager of a coffee estate at Mercara in Coorg, Karnataka. He headed there. In a fortnight, he was sent to one of their friends' estates in Chickmagalur to serve as assistant to the estate superintendent there. His world was one of coffee-plants and the estate's tribal workers. On weekends, there would be a get-together in one of the nearby estates, with the staff of all the neighboring estates. In this way, a year passed. But then Srinivas began feeling a sort of restlessness; he felt that he was cut-off from the modern world.

One day, a young gentleman came to stay for a few days in the estate bungalow. In the evenings, Srinivas used to go to see him and the two of them used to have some pleasant talks. He came to know that the person was the brother of the owner of the estate. He worked in Saudi Arabia and was now on vacation. He had come here to spend a few quiet days away from the crowd. He told Srinivas that a young, educated person like him shouldn't waste his life working on a coffee estate. That he should go out into the world and look for opportunities. He said that in case Srinivas was interested in looking at opportunities in the Gulf States, he had a friend who was a general manager at BP Indian Agencies in Bombay, who were recruiting agents for countries around the Gulf. He said he could give Srinivas a letter of recommendation.

Srinivas was delighted and took the letter before the owner's brother left. In a fortnight, he had given a month's notice to the management of the estate. At the end of the notice period, he left his job and went home. A week later, he was in Bombay.

There he met Mr. Nicholas Caldeiro, an Anglo-Indian from Goa who was the general manager of BP Indian Agencies in Bombay. Srinivas gave the man the letter given to him by his friend. This was back in the time when the city was still Bombay. It had not yet become Mumbai. Mr. Caldeiro, after reading the letter, looked at Srinivas and said that his experience at the coffee estate was not enough to get him a job in the Gulf. He advised Srinivas to meet him after working a couple of years in Bombay. Disappointed, Srinivas left his office. He decided to try his luck in Bombay.

Through some friends, he was able to get a temporary job at a contractors' firm. In about one year, he had moved to an export company. All the while, he felt the importance of education and the necessity of completing his degree. He enrolled at an evening college and completed his B.Sc. On doing that, he shifted to a job at an organic chemicals manufacturing company. After joining the chemical company, he enrolled for a part-time course with the Department of Chemical Technology at Victoria Jubilee Technical Institute (VJTI) – now known as Veeramata Jeejabai Technical Institute – and pursued a B.Sc(Tech-Chemical) course. His working with a chemicals manufacturing company came in handy while doing the course. His past struggles had taught him to look for opportunities wherever available.

Beginnings

By this time, he had been able to build a pretty good network of friends and contacts in Bombay. With the help of one such person, he was able to get into India's Atomic Energy Establishment. He had just completed his B.Sc. Tech (Chem) as well. He joined the Nuclear Reactor Operations division at Canada-India Reactor (now known as the Bhabha Atomic Research Centre) as a trainee junior scientific officer.

Canada-India Reactor (CIR), as the name suggests, was built by the Canadians under an agreement between the governments of India and Canada known as Colombo-Plan. It is a 40 MW, Uranium fuelled, heavy-water moderated, research oriented reactor. Material testing, Isotopes production and breeding U-233 material into fuel grade Uranium (U-235–238) were all part of its main functions. Dr. Homi Bhabha was the director of the government's Atomic Energy Department. Being one of the largest (at that time) and high-power research reactors of the world, scientists from many countries came there with Dr. Bhabha to conduct various experiments. The job of the operating personnel of the reactor was to run the reactor at the various parameters as set by those scientists. The reactor and other establishments of the DAE (Department of Atomic Energy) were housed in a vast complex at a strategically situated area in a place called Trombay, in the outskirts of Bombay.

Srinivas was happy. He had a comfortable, respectable job and a pay that was quite decent in those days. Ever since he'd first started earning, he had made it a point to send a part of his earnings back home, to his elder brother, Ramdas. Though he was comfortable working in Mumbai, he made sure he met and kept in touch with his friend at BP Indian Agencies, a liaison office of British Petroleum in India. BP Indian Agencies functioned as the official recruitment agents for the Kuwaiti Government as well, among other things. One day, a letter came from Mr. Caldeiro saying that a team of officials from the government of Kuwait was there for the recruitment of domain experts in various fields. Mr. Caldeiro said he could assist Srinivas, in case he still had any interest in going to Kuwait. Srinivas had in fact discussed the matter with his friend only a short while ago, just before joining up at the reactor, saying that he would very much like to get a job abroad. His seniors at DAE dissuaded him from leaving, saying that he was young and could go a long way in his field if he stayed with DAE, and that life in the Arabian Gulf was tough, that the weather was severe and inhospitable. It took some time for Srinivas to analyze the various factors and take a decision. The attraction of a lucrative remuneration several times higher than what he was drawing now proved irresistible in the end. He decided to accept the job in Kuwait and informed his friend, Mr. Caldeiro, of his willingness. By that time it had already become a little late and many of the most attractive positions had been filled. One opening was left in the ACHV (air-conditioning, heating & ventilation) section. Thanks to his training at CIR, Srinivas had some theoretical training in this field. But he did not have much practical experience. Moreover, that was not a line of his choice. Srinivas discussed this with his friend, who advised him to take the opportunity for now and then perhaps switch to another line later. So Srinivas resigned from DAE and left for Kuwait in July 1962.

It was mid-July – the peak of summer in Kuwait. Outside temperatures rose up to 55 degrees Celsius during the day and it became difficult to travel or live without air-conditioning, in a vehicle or in a residence. The weather and the environment were totally new to Srinivas.

THE KUWAIT DAYS

Kuwait had been a British protectorate from 1899 to 1961. It had just become an independent nation and a constitution was established in 1962. The first elections to the National Assembly were held soon after. Subsequently, Kuwait joined the Arab League and the United Nations. Neighboring Iraq was hostile and was not prepared to accept it as an independent country. The then-dictator of Iraq, Abdul Karim Kassim, declared that Kuwait was a part of Iraq, its Governorate, and said that he would soon be marching to Kuwait to have lunch with the ruler of Kuwait – who according to him was his governor – and discuss modalities of administration under Iraq. Determined to maintain its independence, Kuwait entered into a defense pact with Britain. This deterred the Iraqis, for a while. Shortly afterwards, Abdul Karim Kassim was assassinated in an internal coup and a new government was installed in Iraq. From then on, there was no significant hostility between the two countries for a long time, not until Saddam Hussein, then president of Iraq, invaded Kuwait in 1990.

Oil was discovered there by the British and operations were being handled by Kuwait Oil Company (KOC) – comprised of the Gulf Oil Corporation of the USA (presently Chevron) and the Anglo-Iranian Oil Company of the UK (presently BP) – before Kuwait's independence.

KOC established a refinery in Kuwait to cater to the local requirements of petroleum products, and made its first export of crude oil in 1946.

Gulf Oil – the Anglo-American consortium – was invited for oil exploration by the then-Amir, Sheik Ahmad Jaber Al-Sabah, a visionary and able administrator whose foresight laid the foundations for the modern welfare state of Kuwait. The Kuwaiti government was getting a royalty at that time, which subsequent wise rulers used for the development of Kuwait and the welfare of its people. It was Abdulla Salem Al-Sabah, later known as the "father of modern Kuwait," who invited international contractors to prepare a blueprint for the overall development of the country and its citizens – including housing, infrastructure, education, healthcare, industry and employment. Subsequent rulers followed the same path and enhanced the development works. Thus, Kuwait became one the most developed welfare states, ahead of all its neighboring Arabian Gulf States in those days. The oil business was still in the hands of the consortium (KOC) though. Kuwait started investing in the shares of the company.

Thanks to the successful nationalization of the Suez Canal in 1957–58 by the Egyptian president Gamal Abdul Nasser, and his famous "Erfa Raas" or "raise your head" slogan, a sort of nationalism began emerging among the Arabs. Kuwait started increasing its share of investment in KOC and in 1970 it started negotiating for a complete takeover of all oil-related business – exploration, downstream operations, marketing and export. The whole process of negotiation and the total takeover lasted a few years and finally, in 1975, Kuwait completely nationalized the country's oil operations. This gave a boost to the economy and from there started the saga of modern Kuwait.

Srinivas found the weather conditions in Kuwait hard to work in. Plus the country was alien to him. Also, the treatment of expatriates by their Arab supervisors was far from acceptable. Back in those days, the image of Indians abroad was very poor. Some Arabs thought those who came to work in their country were coming only because there was no work back in India – which they perceived to be a very poor country. And some of the Indians there contributed to this perception too, by stooping down to the level of slaves. Srinivas came to know that even some officials at the Indian Mission (the country had no embassy there at the time, only a consulate) went out of their way to help some natives in order to get favors from them in return – even at the cost of sidetracking the citizens and bending rules

Srinivas and a colleague, Robert Gomes, a fellow Indian from Bombay, decided to revolt against this behavior and work environment. They talked to the supervisor about his arrogant behavior and asked for some improvements in the working conditions. They said that until these were corrected, they would not take orders from him. This infuriated him. He had been working in that plant for over a decade and two Indian boys were telling him what to do! He prepared a report complaining about them and sent it to the ministry. The next day, the two of them were called to the ministry and told that they were suspended from duty and were not to report until further notice. Some Indians who had been living there for a few years, working in the government departments, told them that the ministry was preparing to send them back home. Untroubled by such comments, Srinivas and his friend just enjoyed not having to work for a while.

Srinivas had a close friend named Ronald Andrews. "Ronie," as Srinivas called him, said the two of them shouldn't just keep quiet and accept whatever the ministry imposed on them. He said they should do something before they were sent back, to make sure other workers did not have to face such a situation. They decided to meet the consul-general of India and report the matter, tell him how they had been treated, about the working conditions they'd faced after having been given a colorful picture of Kuwait when they'd been recruited in India and so on. The consul-general of India at that time was Roy Axel Ghan, a bold and straightforward diplomat with a reputation for helping citizens. He heard them out and asked them to meet him again after three days. A couple of days after this meeting, Srinivas and Robert were called by the director of the Civil Service Commission which looked after employees' affairs in all government ministries. He asked them both to report for duty immediately, but in different places. Srinivas was sent to the control and research laboratory of the power and water production station while Robert went to the central mechanical maintenance centre. This was a welcome change and Srinivas continued to work there for about four years. Robert, after three years there, migrated to the UK and, along with a job there, continued to study engineering.

Kuwait was in the process of establishing its first petrochemical complex in technical collaboration with an American company. This, in fact, was the first petrochemical complex in the region. In a few years though, several states in that region followed suit. Srinivas decided to try his luck there and, with his background, he was able to get into the project. He resigned from the ministry and joined the petrochemical company.

Before leaving the job at the power and water production stations' control and research laboratory, a few colleagues decided to form a private company to be engaged in technical services, meant to cater to the local small industries, which were springing up in large numbers at that time. The team comprised of the head of that section, an Englishman named Dr. Tom Temperly, a Kuwaiti, Mr. Abbas Salim Al-Shatti, and three Indians, including Srinivas. All of them were working in the same section. Government jobs were only up to 1 PM, and there was plenty of spare time for the activities of the private technical services company. The activities, mainly, were inspection of the process and utilities equipments for corrosion, scale formation and so on; and also devising a scheme for the chemical control of these, including systematic periodical analysis of the fluids and supplying the necessary chemicals for the control and treatment.

Although Srinivas had joined the new petrochemical complex, he continued to be an active member of the private firm that they'd started. Over a period of two years or so, their technical services company had a number of permanent clients and grew beyond the boundaries of Kuwait. During a periodical meeting, it was decided that there had to be one permanent fulltime manager to handle the affairs of the company. The team unanimously decided that Srinivas should resign his job with the petrochemical company and take over as manager of the operations of their own technical services company. Apart from his share as a partner, it was decided also that he would be allowed a compensation equivalent to what he was drawing presently at the petrochemical company.

Srinivas resigned from the petrochemical company and took over the fulltime responsibility of managing the technical services company's operations. The growth of the company was remarkable. His Kuwaiti colleague and partner, who was designated the managing director of the company, had an old expatriate friend to whom he was obliged in certain ways. This person had left Kuwait and gone back to his country. The Kuwaiti partner said that he would like to get him back since he was quite proficient when it came to looking after accounts. He wanted this old partner to look after the administration of the company while Srinivas handled the technical services aspect of it. This was agreed to by all the other partners. The Kuwaiti partner's old colleague's name was Baiiju.

Baiiju and the Kuwaiti partner, Mr. Al-Shatti, had been friends for a long time. Baijju was also an ambitious man and wanted to control everything. Taking advantage of his closeness with the Kuwaiti partner, he started working to create a misunderstanding between Srinivas and the other partners. Since all the other partners were working with the ministry Baiiju found that Srinivas was the only obstacle to his achieving his purpose. The misinformation and misunderstanding created by him was so severe that the working atmosphere at the company became tense. There was no friendly communication between the partners. Srinivas stepped back and assessed the situation. So far, he had been sincerely working, and it had reflected in the growth of the company. If he continued working there, he would work the same way he always had and help make the company even more prosperous. But he knew what game Baiiju was playing. He realized that he would have to quit one day, and so he decided to quit before the situation got any worse.

Kuwait, at that time, was a small place. A few developed pockets existed, the population was quite small, industries numbered only a handful and it was generally peaceful. Srinivas was known to a few good people; both expatriates as well as natives. After leaving the technical services company, through a mutual friend, Srinivas was asked by a Kuwaiti gentleman, who was working at a government department, if he would like to start a business in partnership with him. The man confessed that he didn't know much about doing business, but said that he would lend support financially as and when needed and that it would be up to Srinivas to select the line of business and build it up. In those days, no expatriate was allowed to do business independently, without the sponsorship or partnership with a citizen of the country.

The two of them worked out an agreement, registered the firm and decided to start operations after Srinivas returned from a short vacation.

BACK HOME

Srinivas went home on a vacation. It was his third vacation after going to Kuwait. Much before Srinivas left for Kuwait, Ramdas, his elder brother, had gotten married. He now had two children. During his second vacation, Srinivas got married. It was an arranged marriage, to a girl from a family well-known in that area. There had been relations between the two families for generations. The family was known to have large holdings of land and was well-respected by the local feudalistic farm holders in those parts. Rich in their own way, self-sufficient and not placing much value or care for education or the world around, or people outside the realm of their interactions, the children raised by the family, of that generation, all upheld the same view. Perhaps Ramdas chose a girl from this family because Srinivas was an unselfish, carefree person who was always concerned for the well-being of family members, and helped anyone who needed it. Maybe he felt the girl would become a support to him later.

Srinivas was glad to find everyone back home happy, healthy and active. Ramdas had bought some land and property in the family's name. The family had begun to wear the look of affluence and there was respect for them from all around the neighborhood and from their relatives too.

Back home

Srinivas felt that all his struggling and sending money back had paid off. Since the remittance was being made in the name his elder brother, Ramdas, Srinivas' elderly parents and the children of the family were under the impression that Ramdas was taking care of them all by himself. Ramdas himself took special care to cultivate just such an impression in the family and neighborhood. After he had returned from his holidays, Srinivas received a letter saying the marriage of his sister had been fixed and that some extra money was needed. This request was complied to with pleasure.

BACK TO WORK

The operation of the new company was started. Srinivas chose a specialized line of activity for the company – the supply of industrial equipment like heat exchangers, pressure-vessels, towers, specialized control valves, spares, and process chemicals mainly for the petroleum, and other manufacturing industries. Soon, he made a trip to Europe and the Far East with Abu Ali, his Kuwaiti business partner, and garnered the agencies of some good companies as sole representatives for Kuwait. Some of these companies are well reputed in their fields and their products that were well accepted by Kuwait's petroleum industry. Since Srinivas had been working earlier in petrochemical industries and in the ministry, he was fully aware of what kind of products were preferred by these organizations and, on that basis, the companies were chosen for representing.

In a year's time, the company became stabilized and started making money. Of the principals they chose to represent, one Belgian company, Francois de Hondt S.A., was doing good business with Kuwait at that time. The company specialized in the manufacture of heat exchangers of all kinds, in special metals and alloys including spare tube bundles. They were reputed worldwide in their field. And Kuwait imported new exchangers and spares regularly. Many a time, Srinivas had to go several times a year to discuss certain important points relating to the project before preparing quotations and proposals by the principals. Since a lot of business was coming in for them from Kuwait, Srinivas was always given a warm welcome whenever he went. He was received at the airport by the company's chairman, and put up in hotels like the Brussels Hilton or Sheraton. Meetings were always cordial and he used to be invited to dinner at some of the best restaurants in the area. Brussels, being the headquarters of the European Union, was considered as a very expensive city, but Srinivas never felt any pinch since the hotel bills and everything else were paid for by the company and debited in their annual commission account.

Another company which they used to do good business with was Gulde Regalarmaturen K.G. It was a German company based in Ludwigshafen which specialized in manufacturing control valves for petrochemicals, refineries and such. During his business visits, the company made it a point to organize some sightseeing trips for Srinivas. One of such occasions, he was taken to the Heidelberg University and Museum where he had the chance to see some very ancient Sanskrit books and manuscripts.

The business was going well. The office which had once been manned solely by Srinivas – acting as manager, clerk, accountant, salesman and everything else – was now staffed with a secretary, an office manager, sales executives and a part-time accountant. Operations were also moved to a prominent modern building. The company was maintaining a good relationship with all its principals as well as the local customers, attending to all their problems and emergencies. It quickly built up a good reputation for itself in the business community.

It was at this time that the Director of the refineries of Syria called Abu Ali to participate in the rebuilding of the Homs refinery which had been damaged after Israeli bombing. Srinivas and Abu Ali visited Syria subsequently and then of course Srinivas left for Europe. After his discussions with the Italian company, Srinivas moved on to other countries in Europe and obtained offers in line with the desires of the director of the refineries of Syria. All this took him about two weeks. Abu Ali had gone back to Kuwait by this time. Upon getting back, the director appreciated the work done by Srinivas and told him that it would take a few days to study the offers and that he could go back home, in the meanwhile, and wait for their call. Srinivas went back to Kuwait. The call from Damascus never came.

Investigation by Abu Ali's sources in Syria revealed that the Italian company, with which Srinivas had negotiated with first, had sent a team to Damascus. They had met the director and his colleagues and told them that the company could do the whole job on a turnkey basis, and safeguard their interests in an enhanced way. The refinery officials could justify with the government that they would be dealing with only one company instead of various suppliers, which could help avoid delays.

Some Italian companies, back in those days, had an ill-reputation of being unreliable, unethical and opportunistic. Srinivas remembered what he had read in a recent issue of a respectable magazine, the monthly psychology review "*Riza Psychosomatica*." The magazine had said that 70 percent of Italian men and women interviewed had confessed to telling between five and ten lies a day. "Don't worry, it's all been taken care of," was the most common lie told, the publication said. It was no wonder this Italian company had breached the trust of the firm of Abu Ali and Srinivas. Abu Ali said that they had to write-off the expenses and trouble taken as a "business loss."

The part-time accountant at the firm was a Syrian Arab, a distant relative of Abu Ali on his wife's side. He got the good salary usually given to a man in such a post, in those days, in that area. But the man began to get jealous of the amount that Srinivas, an Indian, was getting by way of his profit-share every year. He gradually started flattering Abu Ali, saying he was the "boss" of such a reputed firm. Abu Ali was not very well-educated, though he was a very mature person who held a respectable position in a government organization, a bank that had been engaged exclusively in giving loans to Kuwaitis for house construction, marriage and education etc. Srinivas started to feel that the flattering of the accountant was getting into Abu Ali's head, for Abu Ali had started conducting and projecting himself in a different manner. Srinivas never showed that he noticed such a difference and just ignored the accountant and his activities. It had been five years now since the company had started its operations, and also since Srinivas had last gone on vacation though he had gone to India a couple of times on business.

During one of their trips, Abu Ali had taken his wife and three children to see places in India. This was during the 1970s, when some Kuwaitis, the ones who were not so well-educated or widely travelled, used to think that India was a country of poor people and that was why they always went abroad seeking jobs. Srinivas and Abu Ali's enterprise was representing an Indian company owned by a well-known Marwari industrial family with whom they were doing good business. Srinivas informed them that Abu Ali's family would be accompanying them to see India. And added that he would appreciate it if they could do something to change their view that India was a poor, job-seekers' country.

When they arrived at Delhi, a VIP reception was waiting for them complete with garlands, bouquets and so on. They were taken to the Hotel Claridges where a lavish suite was booked for Abu Ali's family and a room for Srinivas. Each meal was at a different restaurant – in the Ashoka Hotel, the Oberoi, the Leela and other similar places. The visitors were taken to the head office of the Indian company for official discussions. Then the chairman, the owner of the group, invited them all to dinner at his residence in Hauz Khas, a wealthy area of Delhi. His office had drawn up a detailed itinerary for the guests which included visits to places of interest in Delhi and its suburbs, Agra, Jaipur, Udaipur and Ajmeer as well as Srinagar in Kashmir. A dinner in honor of the Kuwaiti family was also arranged at the Oberoi Intercontinental. The Kuwaiti ambassador was the guest of honor. The Kuwaiti ambassador turned out to be a former schoolmate of Abu Ali and the visitors enjoyed the evening immensely. As expected, their views about Indians and their country started changing slowly. And their subsequent visits to India helped accelerate the process. The company arranged for one of its managers to escort the guests and gave instructions to its local offices, in all the places on the itinerary, to make local staff available for the purpose of accompanying the visitors and showing them around.

In Srinagar, after visiting places in and around the city, they all decided to go to Gulmarg. A car drove them up to the base camp. And from there they took a special vehicle, a mini-van with tires wound with barbed chains so as to have grip over ice-covered roads. They all enjoyed watching people ice-skating and riding on carts drawn by dogs. It was almost dark when they all decided to head back. On the way back, the vehicle broke down. They all had to get down and walk through the ice-covered roads. It was a night of ample moonlight and one could only see ice all around. For the Kuwaiti family with three children aged fourteen, twelve and eight, it was a nightmare to walk at night in that strange place. They seemed to be a bit scared. But they had confidence in Srinivas and the man from Delhi who started singing some songs and doing funny dances to ward off their fear. Finally, the lady and children said they could not walk anymore and sat by the side of the road.

Luckily, in a few minutes, they saw a jeep coming down the road. Srinivas stopped it. It was full of Indian Army officers in uniform going for some official party downtown. Srinivas told them about the breakdown of their vehicle and the plight of the foreign family who were not accustomed to walking such long distances and who were now tired and not able to proceed. Two of the officers volunteered to get down so that the jeep could accommodate the lady and children and take them to the base camp. It was decided they would wait there until these two officers and the rest got there on foot. At first, the Kuwaiti family was reluctant to get into the jeep, but Srinivas and the others convinced them that they would be safe and that there was nothing to worry about. They drove off. The rest of the party, half-walking and half-running through that ice-covered road in the moonlit night, though tired, reached the base camp about forty-five minutes later. Mrs. Abu Ali and the children were waiting in the car for Abu Ali and Srinivas. And the officers in the jeep, for their colleagues. Srinivas and the group thanked the officers, who accepted it in their usual sporting spirit.

Next morning, when he came down for breakfast, Srinivas learned that a group of Bollywood stars were staying in the same hotel, and that they would be coming down soon to go to their shooting location. This was when Rajesh Khanna was ruling Bollywood. The group consisted of Rajesh Khanna, Asha Parekh, Tanuja and Joy Mukerjee.

Srinivas told them about the visiting family and said that they would like to take a few photographs with them. The actors gladly agreed and came out and stood with the family and took a few snaps. Abu Ali and his family were thrilled. These photos and the Gulmarg adventure were among the many things about India that they talked about back home, for years, during their community get-together, *Diwaniyat*.

After visiting Calcutta, they came to Bangalore. In those days, there were no flights from Bangalore to Mangalore. They made the journey by car from Bangalore via Mercara. The children, upon seeing the forests and the Ghats on the way, got so excited that they started jumping and crying in the car. They were seeing such forests and coffee estates for the first time. Srinivas left them at a hotel in Mangalore and went home for a couple of days. The family liked Mangalore, a small town where they could walk around and do a little shopping. Upon Srinivas' return from home, and after a day's break in Bombay where the company official received them, they flew back to Kuwait.

In a month, Srinivas' own children would begin their holidays. Srinivas decided to take a long vacation. Now he was the father of four children. Two of them were at school in Ooty in Tamil Nadu. The other two were living with him and his wife and going to school in Kuwait. During the school holidays, they went on a long vacation, leaving Abu Ali to take care of the office along with his accountant.

BUYING A COFFEE ESTATE

Srinivas learnt that his family had become quite respectable in their area and that all his brothers and sisters had been accepted into the society. All his sisters had been married to promising youngsters in good families. His younger brother Srijay was a bit of a rebel who had discontinued his studies while in high school and was doing a technical course with a view to start a self-employment venture. His other brother Kiran had just completed a diploma in Instrumentation Engineering and was looking for an opening. Srinivas had a friend, a flight engineer for Air India, whose relative owned an aircraft maintenance company in Bombay. He talked to him and arranged for an opening in that organization for Kiran. His Air India friend told him that Kiran would be taken as an unpaid apprentice in the instrumentation section, and that the apprenticeship would be for three years. Srinivas agreed and arranged for his brother's stay in Bombay and also started sending him enough money to cover his expenses during that time. After completing the apprenticeship, Kiran was taken to Kuwait and fixed up with the MEW's power stations through Abu Ali, as an instrumentation engineer. Also, the youngest sister's husband, who was not properly employed though he was an automobile engineer, was taken to Kuwait and fixed up with Kuwait

Airways, in its components and control department, through another Kuwaiti friend of Srinivas'. Srinivas used to send money to his elder brother, Ramdas, as and when he asked for it citing reasons such as the marriage of sisters, certain purchases, educational needs of the brothers and sisters, improvement of the home and so on. Besides, in order to boost the name of the family, he had opened a partnership firm with all the brothers and sisters as partners. It was named after the family. He also arranged for the representation of a couple of Bombay-based companies for that area, for the distribution of their products. Ramdas was installed as chief executive of the firm which, over the years, became one of the leading suppliers of certain drugs and diagnostic lab chemicals in the area.

Some money was still left with him and Srinivas decided to invest it in some property. Since a coffee estate was where his career had started, he decided he would buy and invest in a coffee estate. By that time, his relative in the Mercara coffee estate had retired and settled in Chickmaglur. Through him and some of his friends, a 75-acre coffee estate with 50 acres of CRC (Coffee Registration Certificate) plus about 30 acres of *kharab* land (government land without any current ownership) was bought. Srinivas installed this relative as its manager and his rebellious brother Srijay as his assistant. The estate was bought from a Coorgi family, Mr. Kalappa and his sons.

Buying a coffee estate

During those days, coffee estates were largely controlled by the government. An area planted with coffee had to be registered. Before picking the coffee berries, permission from the Central Excise Department had to be obtained, and everyday's pick had to be reported to their office. Dried coffee beans were to be sold only to government approved curers and payment would come only over a period of two to four years. It was not a wise investment (as was proved later) when compared to some other options, but it was not simply the desire for profit that made Srinivas purchase the estate.

Mr. Uthappa, the eldest son of Mr. Kalappa, did not have a good relationship with the rest of the family. He was a senior executive at a private insurance company in Hassan and was living there, about hundred and fifty kilometers away from the estate. He had not agreed to the sale of the estate, which Srinivas didn't know at the time or, rather, was just not told about by the family. Later, when Kalappa's family had left the house in the estate and Srinivas had put his people up there, Uthappa threatened the manager, Srijay and the other staff with dire consequences if they didn't leave the estate in a week's time. The manager, the retired relative of Srinivas, got scared and left the place as he knew that Coorgis were tribal warriors who could be bold and ferocious and could make good on their threats. Kalappa's family assured that they would pacify the eldest son and that no harm would befall anybody. In the place of the relative who had left, Kalappa sent his youngest son, Devayya, to look after the affairs of the estate and train Srijay. There were two labor lines (quarters) and about fifteen families living on the estate and working through the year. Since Uthappa had refused to take his share of the sales proceeds, Kalappa deposited the amount in a bank, in the name of his grandchildren.

Still, the threat of Uthappa was very much there. He declared that he would shoot Srinivas if he sets foot on the estate. Srinivas thought that if he had the courage to buy a property in such a remote place, he would surely be able to protect it as well. One day, he drove to the residence of Uthappa and told him that he had come to have a drink and lunch with him and his family. Uthappa was a little confused to see him there at his home. But Coorgis are generally proud, honest, bold and very hospitable to guests, and so he reluctantly called Srinivas in and asked him to sit down. Srinivas asked him what his problems were, what he could do to help solve these and why he was threatening him. Uthappa opened up and said he had grown up in that family house, that every coffee plant there had been cultivated by him and his father. He said his attachment to the place was so strong that he could not imagine being deprived of it and somebody else taking it over. Moreover, he had never been consulted about the selling of the estate. Srinivas realized that the problem was sentimental and said that he shouldn't think that it was taken over by somebody and that he would always be welcome at the estate as a family member. Since it was purchased now Srinivas said he had to look after the estate and needed his cooperation as well. Srinivas gave him a choice. He told him he could either return the money and take his property back, or else he -should extend his full cooperation and goodwill and help make the estate the pride of the area so that he could one day say that, before Srinivas bought it, it had been owned by him and his family. They had a couple of drinks, made a lot of small talk and had a good lunch. Srinivas left that place then with the satisfaction that he now had a good friend in place of an enemy who had been out to shoot him.

A CHANGE OF JOB

After the long vacation, Srinivas got back to Kuwait. Business was going well back there as he had streamlined everything before leaving. There were some developments though which needed his attention. One important principal had asked for some specific details about a forthcoming expansion project; questions like who the consultants were, when the request for quotation was likely to come up and the possible competitors for them. Such information was not publicly available, but Srinivas got these using his contacts. Because of such factors he was considered an important person by some principals. Also, whenever clients had some technical problems, they called Srinivas to get an answer, hence doing away with all the red tape and delay. Thus, he was relied on heavily by both principals and customers.

A change of job

Abu Ali had never interfered in or questioned Srinivas' doings, though he was kept informed of the important activities that were taking place at the office. Recently though he had started asking to see all the mail that was coming in and going out and all the phone calls that were being made and received. He started imposing various restrictions on the staff at the suggestion of the accountant, which Srinivas obviously didn't like.

There was actually some talk at the time that several leading firms had been originally started by Kuwaitis in partnership with expatriates, mostly Indians, as modest ventures which had bloomed into large business houses with sizeable turnovers and profits. And quite often, a relative who didn't have anything else to do, or an expatriate Arab descending as an advisor, slowly turned the Kuwaiti against his Indian partner. The main issue they brought up was the initial contract, which had usually been instituted when there was not much income to the firm. The Kuwaiti partner would have agreed to a certain percentage of profit, which would later become significant. When the company grew, the share of profit became substantial – enough to kindle the envy of a jobless relative or another expatriate Arab advisor. These people would then slowly worm their way into the business and resort to some ways, including humiliating him, which would make the non-Kuwaiti partner leave the partnership business. Srinivas started sensing that something of the sort was going on here as well.

During that time, the region's first electrical and telecommunication cables manufacturing company was being set up in Kuwait. It was a joint sector venture. Srinivas wanted to explore the possibility of supplying raw materials, mainly insulation material, to the company. The company was functioning in a temporary premises, not far from the office of Srinivas. The Ministry of Electricity, the major shareholder of the company, deputed a senior engineer, sent for training with BCCI, a leading cables manufacturing company in the UK, and installed him as chairman of the new company. A factory was under construction by Furukawa Electric company of Japan, who were the technical collaborators, in the industrial area, which was about twenty-five kilometers from Kuwait City.

Srinivas met the chairman, who explained that specifications for the raw materials had not yet been received from the consultants, Preece, Cardew and Rider(PCR). But he asked Srinivas to keep in touch with him. Besides, they still had to enunciate a purchase procedure. Whenever they met, the chairman used to talk a lot about general business. One day, he finally said that they had got a list of some items and that he would like to get offers for these items within a week. Srinivas got three offers for each item in about four days and presented them to the chairman.

After going through the offers, he asked Srinivas bluntly; "Would you like to join this company?" Srinivas thought he was joking and replied; "Why should I? I am already with a company where I get a good salary and a good share of the profit. If you are looking for staff, just give an advertisement in the local newspaper. I'm sure many people will be interested."

"I know. But I am looking for somebody with managerial level experience, to assist me. If you are interested, just tell me your terms."

A change of job

Srinivas realized he was serious and replied: "I haven't thought about leaving my present job. I have to think about it."

"That's fine. But don't take too long. I need an answer by tomorrow."

Srinivas went to his office and started thinking about the pros and cons of the proposal. He had been feeling uneasy in the office for some time now, with the changed atmosphere, and the accountant's constant flattery of Abu Ali which had gone to Abu Ali's head. Srinivas had in fact lost interest of late in taking up new projects and in discussing such things with Abu Ali. He thought about the proposal of the chairman of the cable company and felt that a change might be a good idea.

The next day, he met the chairman and presented his terms. The chairman accepted his terms and asked when he would be able to join. Srinivas said he would require two months to relinquish his present responsibilities, arrange for a successor in Abu Ali's firm and settle the accounts. The chairman said that was too long and asked him to make it as soon as possible – a month at the most. He also said that Srinivas should come in when he had some spare time and attend to some of the pending commercial aspects.

Srinivas told Abu Ali that he had decided to quit and that the sooner he was relieved the better. Abu Ali was shocked, but he did not persuade Srinivas to stay – maybe because the accountant had brainwashed him saying that he would save a lot of money, which he otherwise had to pay as Srinivas' share of the profit. Abu Ali asked Srinivas to arrange for a successor to himself, and to go to the Far East with him to acquire agency rights for some consumer items which he thought he could market by himself in some cooperative societies (supermarkets at various residential districts which he was on friendly terms with the management by virtue of his position in a government bank that gave credit to Kuwaiti citizens to form such cooperatives). Srinivas agreed.

During his last vacation, his elder brother Ramdas had asked him to find an opportunity for his son-in-law who held an engineering diploma and was working for the Public Works Department as a junior engineer. Srinivas thought that this person could be okay for Abu Ali. He decided to contact some of the principals and arrange for a week's training for him, to familiarize with their products and services. Accordingly, he called some of the important principals, informed them about his leaving the company, told them about his replacement and asked them to train him for a week or so. The principals agreed. Srinivas informed Ramdas about the arrangements he had made and asked him to keep his son-in-law ready as the visa and tickets would be arranged by the company. Abu Ali was asked to arrange these. Thus, the first requirement of Abu Ali was met. Also, Ramdas was very happy.

Regarding the second one, Srinivas contacted some companies in the Far East. Based on the response, they chose to visit Singapore, Hong Kong and Thailand. They couldn't find anything acceptable in Singapore and so left for Hong Kong. Abu Ali preferred to represent some good manufacturers of crockery, Dinner sets and other such melamine ware items which were just getting popular in

A change of job

Kuwait and the Gulf States. In Hong Kong, they met an Indian businessman who had been living in those parts for over thirty years. He was a World War veteran. After the war, he had become a businessman, dealing in scrapped tanks, airplanes and so on. He had married a Japanese lady, lived in Japan for over twenty years and had now settled in Hong Kong. He happened to be from Srinivas' town originally, from a family well-known to him. After they got to know each other, the businessman, Mr. Ragh, was there to help with anything they needed. They went to a couple of manufacturers, but found that the prices were not attractive. Mr. Ragh suggested that Thailand was cheaper than Hong Kong and that he had a friend there, Mr. Alexander, who owned a chain of jewelry stores, was very actively engaged in social work and was the district governor of Lions Club in Bangkok. He said he would telephone to his friend to guide them. Accordingly, they left for Bangkok.

On reaching the hotel at Bangkok, Srinivas called Mr. Alexander, who confirmed Mr. Ragh's phone call and said that he'd had a stroke recently. His mobility, thus, was hampered and his son and daughter were looking after the activities now. He added that he had a jewelry showroom in the hotel they were staying in, and that his daughter, Ratinavaroja, was looking after it. He said he would phone her up and tell her to take care of them, and they could meet her in the jewelry showroom of the hotel.

They met Ratinavaroja. Besides managing the showroom, she was engaged in social activities as well. On hearing their requirements, she made a few phone calls and then told one of her staff to take them to a factory owned by her friend. It was a melamine factory in the suburbs of Bangkok. They produced a variety of items there – dinner sets, kitchenware and more, in attractive designs. The prices too were much lower than in Hong Kong. They visited the factory and an agreement was made for Abu Ali to be the sole distributor of their products in Kuwait. The next day, they met Nielson, the son of Mr. Alexander, and a gemologist, who looked after the rest of the jewelry stores and sat in the head office in the main business district of the city.

Before even embarking on this trip, Srinivas had attended to some of the files and papers at the cable company. By the time they returned, his accounts were finalized; he left the partnership firm and joined the cable company. Since the factory construction and machinery installation were almost complete, the raw materials and consumables had to be purchased now within a strict timeframe. There were about three hundred items that had to be bought – some in bulk and some in small quantities. The yearly purchase of raw materials and consumables came up to about 500 to 600 million dollars. Srinivas was made the cable company's corporate purchase manager and was responsible for purchases, stores and warehouses.

A tentative commissioning date for the plant was worked out, as was the time when all the raw materials had to reach the warehouses. Accordingly, Srinivas prepared a bar chart, stipulating the various dates for different stages of the purchase process such as completion of sending out quotation requests, tentative shipment dates, the date of arrival at the port of Kuwait from various places and the clearing and transporting time. He and his team strictly

A change of job

adhered to the timeframe and the process was carried out to the satisfaction of all concerned, thus proving Srinivas' ability to carry out such tasks in a remarkable way. The chairman wanted all the materials to come from reputed companies in Europe and Japan. Nothing was to come from India or other eastern countries.

There was an item, a small quantity (five tons) of polyester tapes of various colors, which would be used for identification of cables, especially telephone cables. Along with some German, British, Dutch and Japanese companies, Srinivas sent a quotation request to an Indian company, Garware Polyester & Plastics Ltd. Offers came from the German, British and Japanese companies and from Garware in India. The price given by the Indian company was almost one-fifth of the European and Japanese prices. Purchase decisions were taken by a committee consisting of the chairman, technical Manager and Srinivas. Price comparisons, company names and deviations in specifications if any, were tabulated and discussed. Decisions were made after scrutinizing various merits. When the issue of the polyester identification tapes came up, the chairman insisted on placing the order with a European company in spite of the higher price. Srinivas said that the price difference was too much, that Garware was a reputed company and their product quality was as good as anything international. Mr. Soudring, the technical manager said that he had no problem with an Indian supplier as long as the product strictly met specifications – which Srinivas assured him it would. But the chairman was still hesitant to accept. Srinivas convinced him saying he would make sure the material arrived on time and strictly adhere to the specifications. Finally, the chairman reluctantly agreed and an order was placed with Garware.

Most of the material, everything from copper to special PVC, reached Kuwait on time, but the polyester tapes had not been shipped in spite of reminders. Srinivas was in a panic. The marketing head was not available and no one was able to give him any definite date for shipment. Finally, he got Mr. Garware, the chairman of the company, on the phone and told him that the order had been placed a couple of months ago and that, while all other raw materials had reached Kuwait, they could not start production without polyester tape. The production would have to be suspended until they had the tape, and this would result in huge losses. Mr. Garware understood the situation and said he would arrange to send one ton of product that very day by air by a chartered flight. He also said the balance would be shipped in a week and that it would reach Kuwait around ten days after that. The marketing manager was in the USA on a business trip and hadn't given any clear instruction regarding this shipment, as it was a small quantity. Srinivas' chairman wasn't so confident, but when they received the one ton of product sent by air, he was happy. Garware's marketing manager, Mr. Chowla, visited Kuwait on his way back from the USA and apologized profusely. The chairman was happy with the company and its product and orders for this material were continuously given to them. Srinivas too felt proud that he had found an Indian company that was reliable and living up to its reputation.

A change of job

Srinivas worked in this capacity for about seven years. After the initial years of hectic activity, the work became routine and he started getting restless even though he was comfortable financially. He decided to join up for a business management course with an American University, the Southern California University, as an external student. He completed the program over three years and earned a doctorate in business administration. By this time, he had also completed seven years with the cable company. One day, he came across a group of financial consultants who arranged for large sums of money to finance projects, against prime-bank-guarantees. He found it interesting and decided to leave the cable company and join the group.

To the surprise of his colleagues and the chairman of the company, he resigned from the job, saying that he planned to go back home as his children were growing and needed his personal guidance and attention. The chairman, who always had a soft corner for him, affectionately asked if he had the finances to sustain himself. He said Srinivas was not that old and could have worked for a few more years. But Srinivas went back home, deciding to settle in Bangalore where he had purchased an apartment in a good area. He settled his family there and enrolled his children in good, reputed schools. Bangalore had a reputation as a place with good educational institutions and salubrious weather – though that reputation has much eroded now with the massive influx of people and industries as well as infrastructure bottle-necks.

THE TIMES WITH
THE FINANCIAL GROUP

A brother of his wife, who had just come to Bangalore from his village after getting his B.Com degree, was in search of a job. Srinivas fixed him up as a trainee at a good chartered accountants' firm and arranged for him to stay with him and his family. Srinivas then returned to Kuwait and joined the financial group, which was working on arranging a one billion dollar loan to a Canadian firm – Gold Point Resources, which was engaged in gold mining in Canada. The group had identified a source for the funds: a Trust owned by a prince of the royal family of Saudi Arabia. Negotiations were with the fund-managers of the Trust, based in America and the borrower temporarily based in Geneva, Switzerland, as the transaction was to take place through a fiduciary bank, Compagnie de Banque et d'Investment, in Geneva. And the financial group was in the middle of supervising the preparations and submitting the required documents to the bank. As things progressed, it became necessary for one of the representatives of the financial group to be with the borrower and the fiduciary bank, to facilitate communication and verify the documents on behalf of the trust. The group assigned the task to Srinivas. He went to Geneva and met Mr. Josef Slymovich, the chairman of Gold Point Resources. He was a retired governor of the Central Bank of Canada. He said that he had set up eleven central/reserve banks in Asia, Africa and Latin America and knew as many heads of countries – presidents, kings and prime ministers. Some of them were even very close friends. One of them was Julius Nyrare of Tanzania and he promised to take Srinivas to meet him once the transaction was over. The purpose of this loan he was taking, the chairman said, was to expand his mining operations in Canada and also to expand it to Costa Rica where he had arranged for prospecting minerals and to build up infrastructure in partnership with the government.

Together, Srinivas and he arranged for the required documents and submitted the same to the bank. The trust was informed of this by the financial group in Kuwait. Each of the group's members was to get a commission of one percent of the loan amount, or 10 million dollars each, on disbursement of the loan, and "Irrevocable Pay Orders" were prepared and issued by the bank, signed by its vice-president and the borrower, Mr. Slymovich, and stamped and notarized by an attorney in Geneva. These were then handed over to Srinivas. Slymovich, Srinivas and the bank officials were informed by the financial group that trustees were on their way to Geneva to finalize the transaction, and everybody anxiously waited for them. A week passed, and then the news came that the trustees were in Malta, busy buying a bank for the prince, the owner of the fund, and that it might take a few more days for them to reach Geneva. Another week passed, and still there was no sign of the trustees. Then the news came that they had gone back to the USA and that a fresh date would be announced for their arrival. Srinivas felt it was a clear case of circumvention,

The times with the financial group

where the borrower and the trustees had made direct contact. He figured they might have arranged to meet in some other country, maybe Malta, to avoid paying the middlemen. The financial group called him back to Kuwait, but he decided to try for some business in that area first. He was disappointed by the failure, but his spirit was not dampened.

He went to Paris, a city more familiar to him and comparatively more economical. In the financial group, there was a Somali gentleman named Mohamed Hussein. He was in contact with Srinivas and said there were good business opportunities in Djibouti. Djibouti is a small African country, adjacent to Somalia, on the Red Sea coast, with a capital city of the same name. On the other side of the Red Sea is Yemen, bordered on the north by Saudi Arabia and to the east by Oman.. Mohamed Hussein said he knew some influential people in Djibouti and that they should explore business possibilities there. He asked Srinivas to go there and said that he would meet him there. Djibouti was under French rule earlier, but was now a republic. And there were regular flights to the country from Paris.

Srinivas had by now also formed a consultancy firm by the name of Dr. Srinivas & Associates. Mohamed Hussein and Srinivas met with a business house in Djibouti called International Consultancy Office which was owned by one Mr. Idriss Omar Gulleh. Mr. Idriss was the cousin of the president of that country at the time. They identified some projects they could cooperate on and drafted an agreement to that effect. The first one was a housing project for the defense services of the country. It was a major project, financed by an international organization. The task of finding a suitable Indian company, which would safeguard the interests of all involved on the project, was entrusted to Srinivas. He met and discussed with people from a few companies in Bombay and settled on a medium-sized but competent firm by the name of Shah Constructions based in Worli, Bombay. They had built some marvelous buildings in various parts of the country. It was a family-owned company and the chairman was Mr. Harshvardhan Shah. He was also the president of the All India Builders' Association. After initial discussions, the specifications and details of the project were given and Mr. Sirish. H. Shah, the chairman's son and MD of the company, who was given responsibility for this project. He and the firm's chief engineer decided to come down to Djibouti, along with Srinivas, for a site inspection and to prepare a proposal. In a week, the site visit, the meetings with the concerned officials and the collecting of necessary information were completed and a proposal was finalized by Mr. Sirish Shah and his team. The defense minister of

The times with the financial group

Djibouti personally wanted to meet the contractors, prior to submitting the proposal to his secretariat.

Mr. Idriss Omar Gulleh conducted a small class for Mr. Shah about the temperament of African politicians in general and said that the minister might ask to reduce the price, as it would reflect well on him if it was on the record that he had brought down the proposed price of the project. So he suggested that the price structure be such that a good discount *could* be given when the minister asked for it during the meeting, in the presence of his officials. He added that the discount would not have to be confirmed during the meeting itself, but rather an assurance should be given that the price structure would be reviewed to honor the minister's request for a reduction.

Mr. Shah, his chief engineer, Srinivas and Mr. Idriss Omar Gulleh reached the office of the minister at the appointed time. Besides the minister himself, there were a couple of officials in civilian clothes, the commander-in-chief and two other senior military officials in uniform. The proposal, a 360 million US dollars housing project, to be built at the northern most and southern end of the country, was presented to the minister, who went through it and then passed it on to the commander-in-chief. They asked several technical questions and these were answered by the contractor's team, apparently to the satisfaction of the officials. The minister took back the proposal, went through it again and told Mr. Shah that the price was high and needed reviewing. Mr. Shah was a young American-educated engineer, unfamiliar with the nature and pride of tribal African officials and so, in spite of the advice given by Mr. Gulleh, Shah exploded and said the prices had been worked out very carefully and that there was no way to reduce them any further. Srinivas and everyone else on his side looked at each other, wondering what Mr. Shah was thinking, especially since they had talked to him about this just the previous day. They could see also that the minister was not looking happy. He coolly said that they would study the offer further in a couple of weeks and get back to them. Srinivas and his crew had been expecting a positive reply immediately and that was why Mr. Gulleh had taken the trouble of advising Mr. Shah prior to the meeting. Given Mr. Shah's behavior and remarks, Srinivas and Mr. Gulleh could already predict the outcome and were very disappointed. The next day, Mr. Shah and his chief engineer returned to India. After a week, he called Srinivas more than half a dozen times and said he was prepared to reduce the price even by fifteen percent. But it was too late and Srinivas told him to deal directly with the defense minister if he so wished, as he knew that Shah had already hurt the pride of the minister and would not be given another chance.

These two failures, at Geneva and Djibouti, had taken a big toll on Srinivas in terms of money and effort. Some more business possibilities came in through Mr. Idriss Guleh, but he decided to go home and be with his family for some time, and check on the state of his coffee estate, which Srijay was now fully looking after. For ten years now the coffee estate had been under the management of Srijay. He used to ask for money periodically and Srinivas used to send it to him. Srijay had done some remarkable development work on the estate, but he was not able to break even, leave alone making a profit. And since money was coming in whenever

The times with the financial group

he asked for it, he never bothered with keeping control over the finances. Even after Srinivas left his job in Kuwait, Srijay expected to get money to run the estate. Srinivas installed a financial controller-cum-accountant on the estate, but Srijay didn't like anybody asking questions about the way he spent. And given his temperament, no one was willing to stay there and work for too long. Finally, Srinivas spoke with a bank and sourced some working capital. He asked Srijay to strictly control his finances, telling him that he would have no alternative but to sell the estate otherwise.

BUSINESS IN MUMBAI

Srinivas stayed at home with his family for a few weeks in Bangalore. He began to think that he should find a way to earn some money by utilizing his long and varied experience. Now he had his own business, Dr. Srinivas & Associates. He had an apartment in Mumbai (by now Bombay had become "Mumbai") and an old friend and colleague Mr. Joy Joseph who said he could introduce Srinivas to some businessmen in Mumbai whom he could talk to and maybe find a way to move forward. So Srinivas moved to Mumbai. He saw potential in the export of dyes and pharmaceutical intermediates to Europe and the import of some raw materials too. He decided to use his apartment as a residence-cum-office and start an export-import company under the name of Dr. Srinivas & Associates. He contacted some people he knew in Germany and the Netherlands who initially had some reservations about doing business with an Indian company, but finally, due to their long business relations with Srinivas in Kuwait, agreed to cooperate. Import restrictions and foreign exchange control were severe at the time and Srinivas decided to focus on export more. He exported some consumer items to the Gulf and, in the meantime, worked with a Hamburg-based company which imported intermediate chemicals and supplied to companies like BASF, BAYERS, Glaxo and such.

Srinivas tied up with a small-scale dye-intermediate manufacturer based in Baroda, Gujarat. The company was manufacturing for and supplying to the local market, and when the prospect of export was discussed, Nalin C. Patel, the owner of the company, was thrilled and readily agreed to cooperate. The product sample was collected and sent to the Hamburg contact, Mr. Wolfgang Ladwig. The samples were tested in his client's labs in Germany and found to be substandard and so was not approved. Srinivas requested Mr. Ladwig to get information from his client, BASF, on the process parameters in order to forward these to Mr. Patel, so that he would be able to produce the quality acceptable for them. Mr. Ladwig said that such information was normally classified, but promised to try and get it. In a few days, the details were sent. These were, in turn, passed on to Patel who found that he would need two more additional pieces of equipment so as to fulfill these process conditions. These were installed and the product was manufactured. Samples were collected again and sent to Germany. This time, the quality was found to be acceptable, but Patel was warned that this level of quality had be consistently maintained or else he'd have to face the risk of rejection. Srinivas was then called by Ladwig to Hamburg to finalize a long-term supply contract.

In the meantime, Dr. Srinivas & Associates got an order from Holland for Acetyl Salicylic Acid, a bulk-drug and intermediate for aspirin. The supplier was Sirishma Fine Chemicals & Pharmaceuticals, Bangalore, a public limited company promoted by a relative of a union minister. The Dutch company used to import from Indonesia and had never been interested in importing from India.

Indian suppliers had a very bad reputation at that time. Overseas importers used to say that Indian companies never shipped on the agreed date and asked for extensions of letter of credits several times. They would also provide excellent samples, but the material they shipped would be substandard sometimes. Amidst such criticism, Srinivas got an order for one container of material from the Dutch company along with a promise that, if the shipment got there on time and the quality was as good as the samples', they would place regular monthly orders on a long-term basis.

This was the year 1988–89. There was an acute foreign exchange shortage in India. Import restrictions were very severe. It was the worst years of the "license-raj." Usually, imports were permitted only against exports. So most companies grabbed at opportunities for export, even if prices were lower than what they sold for in the local market. And because of all this, there was a shortage of raw materials for Indian manufacturers. And even if they were available, the prices were substantially higher than international prices. Sirishma Chemicals offered a price comparable to international prices. The delivery period quoted was four weeks from the receipt of the letter of credit.

It was a very crucial order for Srinivas. If this was executed without any hitches, he was likely to get monthly orders from the Dutch company for this material for a long time. So he visited Sirishma Chemicals almost weekly, reminded them of the shipment date and how important it was to supply the material in line with the specifications. The export manager of Sirishma assured him that the quantity that needed to be sent was only two day's worth of their production and that there was nothing to worry about. Shipping was the responsibility of the buyer and they had nominated a vessel sailing from Chennai around that time and told the company to send the material to the warehouse of the shipping company, two days ahead of sailing. The week before the agreed shipping date, the export manager hurriedly called Srinivas and informed him that there had been some problem in the plant. The plant had to be shut down, disrupting production. As a result, he said, they would not be able to meet the shipment date and needed an- urgent extension of the L/C by another month. When Srinivas informed the Dutch company of this, his friend there told him that things had gone exactly as he'd thought they would, and asked him to forget about the order. At Srinivas' insistence though they finally granted the extension Sirishma wanted.

Apart from public and promoters (Chaturvedis), the commerce secretary, an IAS officer, was a director of the company, from the government's side. Srinivas approached him and told him the situation, highlighting the opportunity for long-term export business – which the government was doing all it could to promote. The man assured Srinivas he would do his best to see that the export was made in a satisfactory way. Srinivas was happy and contacted Sirishma who assured him that, this time, they would ship on time. However, as the shipping date neared, the company told him that there had been another major breakdown at the plant and that they had to get the spare parts from the United States. They said they need eight months to a year to restart the plant. This was a false story. What had really happened was that, on the basis of this export order and with their influence in the government, the company had imported huge quantities of raw material, produced, and then sold their product in the local market for five times the export price. In India, quality specifications were not so strict whereas for export, pre-shipment quality inspection was mandatory – and in this case it was to be done by SGS, an international inspection agency that had offices all over the world. Ethics, commitment and such were alien words to these kinds of unscrupulous, corrupt businessmen. When Srinivas contacted the government director, he said he was helpless if the plant had been shutdown and thus washed his hands of the problem. Later, Srinivas came to learn that this director used to get a lot of benefits from the chairman of Sirishma and some favors from the union minister too.

Little did Srinivas know that another even bigger disappointment was waiting for him. He went to his friend and buyer of the chemicals in Hamburg, Mr. Wolfgang Ladwig, in the hope of concluding a long-term purchase contract with him. He had an agreement with Patel's company for supplying the required material at a price which had been accepted by the buyer earlier. When Srinivas got there, Mr. Ladwig said he been offered a cheaper price for similar material from another company. He had even received a sample from them a few days ago, tested it and found it to be okay. He showed Srinivas the price quoted by that company, which was indeed lower than the price Srinivas was offering by about ten percent. The margin he kept with Patel's company was about five or six percent. After the preliminary discussions, they went for lunch and then came back. Mr. Ladwig said he had a visitor waiting for him and would be back in some time. About an hour later, he came back with another man. Srinivas was shocked. The other man was Patel himself! He had sent a fresh sample in the name of another company owned by him, signing as Chimanbhai Patel. And Mr. Ladwig didn't know that he was dealing with the same person Srinivas was. Patel had not expected Srinivas to be there on the same day as him and looked stupefied. He tried to explain, giving Srinivas some unconvincing story about how he had come to Germany for other purposes and then thought of dropping by Mr. Ladwig's office. Srinivas asked why he had made direct contact when he knew Srinivas had spent money, time and a lot of effort on his behalf. Patel said that starting direct dealings with the German company had not been his intention and that they could discuss the details back home. Mr. Ladwig assured that he would not deal directly with Patel as long as Srinivas could match the price.

Reflections of a lone traveller

Srinivas was willing to reduce his margin, but he knew that unless Patel reduced his price he would not be able to match the price Mr. Ladwig had shown him. He went to Patel's factory a couple of times, but Patel was not available. On the phone and in correspondences, he said he could not reduce his price and that he was not dealing with Ladwig's company directly.

Srinivas lost money in his attempt to do business in Mumbai. It was a real blow and he was wondering how he could begin again.

He decided to sell his apartment in Mumbai, wind up his operations there and go back to Bangalore.

THE GRANITE BUSINESS

Srinivas stayed at home for a few days. His coffee estate was still depending on his remittance to pay the laborers as the margin allotted by the bank as working capital had reached its limit, and payment to the bank was from the amount that came, as and when it did, from "curers." Srinivas decided to sell the estate, clear all his liabilities and give some of the proceeds to Srijay so he could establish himself elsewhere, and have some money for his future activities. He had an ad published in the classified column of a popular newspaper, got some offers, selected one and sold the estate. He made about three times the amount he had first invested, twelve years ago. If it had been land or some building in Bangalore, he would have got more than ten times the investment he'd made in 1976. Anyway, he was relieved that he no longer had to give money to the estate every week. He cleared all his liabilities and had some funds in hand, and some peace of mind too.

Things had changed by now. There were no more government restrictions on coffee growers as there used to be earlier, and the coffee could be marketed anywhere the owner liked.

Srinivas was the type who could not stay idle for long and started thinking about what to do next. He realized that in every business he started, he was depending on somebody else's product. He thought of working on a product of his own. After thinking about various options, he finally decided to get into granite quarrying. On the outskirts of Bangalore, there were a lot of areas where granite could be found in abundance and there were a lot of quarries in operation. He talked to a couple of his friends who expressed interest in joining him. They bought an area not far from Bangalore, in Krishnagiri, in Tamil Nadu, where it was confirmed by local experts that a variety of granite called "Paradiso" was available. Exploration was started in full swing, employing experienced workers and heavy machines like excavators, cranes, compressors and so on.

Granite, in those days, were controlled by some powerful lobbyists who believed that might was right. They created a lot of hurdles for newcomers and put out propaganda against them to potential buyers, mainly foreigners. Those who wanted to come down and see the quarry and the product were diverted to the quarries belonging to these lobbyists. Srinivas & Co supplied a few "blocks" to some local companies, but was not able to make any export for a long time. The granite business involves heavy investment and working capital, since laborers and heavy machines were involved. And if the material lay around without getting sold, it took a heavy toll on the owners. One partner of Srinivas' bought a small cutting and polishing factory to produce slabs and tiles, to make and sell finished products, utilizing the raw blocks from the quarry. It was a good idea and everyone else supported and welcomed it. Srinivas decided to let the quarry be taken care of by his two partners. He decided he would buy another quarry near Kanakpura, Karnataka, where another variety of granite known as "Multicolour" was available.

He bought about five and a half acres of quarry land and started working on it. He made arrangements for working capital with a leading nationalized bank. Meanwhile, he met the owner of a leading civil contracting firm based in Mumbai, who showed interest in financing the project on a partnership basis provided half the land was pledged as security. This was agreed to and production work was started. Skilled laborers and heavy machines were hired. Camps were built for the laborers on the site. Production of good "blocks" was started, which had potential to attract any buyer. For transporting the blocks to the port for shipping, permits from the local office of the Mining and Geology Department were needed and these were applied for.

Srinivas decided that he had to somehow make *this* venture a success. An Italian friend of his, Bruno Battelli, suggested that he visit the granite exhibition in Carrara, Italy, where many buyers would set up stalls. Srinivas, he said, could meet them, show them samples of his product and, perhaps, get an order or at least promises from them that they would visit his quarry when they came to India to make purchases or to "mark the blocks" as it was called in the industry. Battelli gave him some introductions as well. Srinivas went for the exhibition in Carrara, met a few good companies who regularly imported from India and got promises that their markers would visit his quarry when they next came to Bangalore. A Florence-based Italian company known to Battelli placed a trial order for fifty cubic meter and promised that, if the material met their expectations, they would visit Srinivas' quarry and place further orders. Srinivas returned from Carrara, jubilantly.

In his absence, one of the representatives of the Mumbai-based construction company was looking after the quarry. Here the lobbyists – or rather the mafia – were much more powerful than in Krishnagiri. They were jealous that somebody from another state was operating a quarry so well, producing so much good material and also securing orders. If allowed, it seemed possible that Srinivas could also become a good exporter – a notion that they could not tolerate. Against the purchase order, on behalf of the company he'd introduced Srinivas to, Battelli marked the blocks for export and Srinivas applied for the transport permits from the Mining and Geology Department. Normally, such permits came in about four or five days. His man went to collect it, but it was not ready even after a week. So Srinivas went to the department and met the senior officer – who told him that his file was not to be seen and that he should apply for a file to be made in his name, which would involve inspection of the quarry by M&G officials again, at their convenience, and getting an environmental clearance. If they approved, a file would be made in his name and Srinivas could apply for the transport permits. All this had been done earlier and a file had already been made, but the official was in no mood to listen to Srinivas' protests, saying the file could not be traced.

Srinivas knew it was the work of the granite mafia. They were so powerful that they could dictate terms to the M&G office of that village. Later on, one among them became a minister in the government of Karnataka, another a MLA and so on. They also made the villagers file a complaint saying that whenever there were blasts in the quarry of Srinivas, (a normal feature in all quarries,) the noise disturbed them. They were also made to say that fragments of stone fell in their fields and damaged their crops even though the fields were at least a few kilometers away from the quarry. Thus, the mafia arranged for a group to give a bad report when the M&G officials visited the quarry. This created a delay in opening the file, getting the license and in exporting. The Florence-based Italian company informed Srinivas that they would cancel the order and withdraw the L/C if there were going to be further delays.

Meanwhile, the Mumbai-based construction company withdrew from the cooperation arrangement and sent a notice saying that whatever they had invested had to be returned in two weeks or they would register half the property in their name as per the agreement. They went ahead, after couple of weeks, and registered the property in their name. The misery of Srinivas was not to end there. He had taken some "packing credit" from the bank against his letter of credit. He had produced enough material and he had it all ready for export, and it was worth five times all the liabilities he had, but unless the M&G's approval came, until the file was opened in his name and he got the license for moving the goods, he could not export or sell anything from the quarry officially. It would require high influence and lots of money to bribe the necessary people – and Srinivas was not in a position to do that, nor did he have any inclination to do so. He thought about it for days and then finally decided to quit the business. He left the remaining land and the blocks produced so far for the bank to auction in order to recover their money. The losses sustained by Srinivas were significant; he had become almost penniless.

SRINIVAS GOES BACK TO KUWAIT

By now, his youngest son had got his engineering degree from the Manipal Institute of Technology and started working in a software company in Bangalore. He was not happy with that though. He wanted to go to the United States and do his MS. Srinivas told him to prepare for that. He started preparing for his TOFEL and writing to various universities. One condition for getting a student visa at that time was that the parent of the student must have a bank balance of at least thirty lakhs, or three million rupees. This was a time when Srinivas was finding it difficult to raise even thirty thousand rupees. However, he told his son not to worry and asked him to prepare.

Srinivas considered various options. He knew that even for the exploring of opportunities, he needed money. He thought of the company that had been started by him in his native town, which was being managed by his brother, Ramdas. He asked Ramdas if there was any money he could spare. Ramdas flatly refused saying the company earned just enough to run itself. In 1975, when he had first started the business, Srinivas had invested 100,000 rupees in it. Now it was 1990. He knew the company had flourished, earned a reputation as a reliable and authentic supplier of diagnostics, lab chemicals equipment, and was doing well. Ramdas and his son were managing the business with adequate staff. Srinivas felt bad about the attitude of his brother and told him that, as per the deed of the partnership, Srinivas was the managing partner. Srinivas also said that he would like to leave the partnership and have his share of the capital back. Though he was evidently happy at Srinivas' leaving the company, Ramdas said he would need to look into the state of the company's finances and get back to him. The next day, he said the company could give Srinivas 50,000 rupees in case Srinivas was willing to leave. He agreed and Ramdas asked to sign some forms and papers. He gave him a cheque of 25,000 rupees and said he would give him the balance in two weeks. Srinivas took the cheque and left.

Srinivas had another commitment to fulfill. When he'd sold the estate, he thought of constructing a modern house on the land of his wife. Presently, there was an ancient building there which had been built some decades ago by her parents. In Bangalore, he had entered into a contract for construction with a local engineer who had a construction company. He visited occasionally and made payments as per the progress and the requests made by the engineer. Then the contractor's father became ill and had to have a major surgery. The engineer took money from a few clients of his and used it for the treatment, and was not able to work on the buildings he was to construct. One day, he closed down his shop and left for Singapore. Srinivas' house was about 90 percent completed when he left. And now his financial situation was such that he would not be able to call somebody else to complete it.

Srinivas was miserable. He had been a very successful businessman in Kuwait, where he had lived and worked for over twenty-four years. But in his own country, he was a failure. He contacted some of his businessmen friends in Kuwait and told them that he was planning to come back. They remembered him as a man who succeeded in whatever business he got into and welcomed him back. He went back to Ramdas for the balance of money, who gave him another 10,000 rupees. Srinivas felt bad about the attitude of Ramdas, but he remembered his father's advice, that he should never try or bother to match someone's meanness.

Soon, Srinivas was back in Kuwait. One of his businessmen friends, through whom he had once got a position for his brother-in-law in Kuwait Airways, welcomed him back. He was dealing in consumer goods and running a travel agency. He wanted to establish a petroleum services division in his company and asked Srinivas to be in charge of it, as its general manager.

Though Srinivas knew the field well, he had not been in touch with the industry – which had grown in leaps and bounds in Kuwait – for over ten years and it was a really challenging job for him. He had not had any contact with the field after leaving Abu Ali. He found that many of the companies once represented by Abu Ali were no more with him. Some companies had now chosen to be represented by other new and aggressive local companies. Some had changed their ownership and some had been acquired by bigger companies. Abu Ali too had almost retired from business by now. Local petroleum companies had expanded.

New refineries and petrochemical plants had come up. And, in many of them, the management was entirely made up of European or American technical collaborators. The systems of administration and procurement and so on were very different from old days too. It was all done entirely at the discretion of the technical collaborators. The way Srinivas saw it, the only way forward was to contact foreign companies whose products were in use in these industries, who did not have any local representation, and convince them that his company could promote and enhance their business and safeguard it in the face of competition. He was able to get the representation of a couple of good American companies and a French company and establish petroleum division for the parent company in a profitable way. Abdulaziz Al-Hogal, the owner of the company was happy. Srinivas too.

Meanwhile, his youngest son had completed his TOFEL, registered with a college under Hartford University in Connecticut, Georgia, and was all set to leave. Srinivas didn't know, for some time, how to handle the situation. Finally, he decided to meet Mr. Abbas Salem Al-Shatti, once his colleague and now the chairman of the technical services company which Srinivas was one of the founding partners of. The company, by now, was well established as an exclusive supplier of water treatment and corrosion control systems and chemicals. It had also entered into the field of supply and installation of distillation plants, cooling systems and boiler plants etc, with an annual turnover of many millions of dollars. The old Partners had all left and Abbas' friend Baiiju had died a couple of years ago. Dr. Temperly had left Kuwait and now ran a consultancy firm of his own in Saudi Arabia. Also, an honorary advisor to this company. Abbas Salem Al-Shatti, was the sole proprietor now.

Srinivas decided to meet him and talk to him about his son. He told him that he was preparing to go to America for his higher studies, and about the condition wherein his parents would have to have a bank balance of three million rupees if he was to get a student visa. Srinivas needed to submit a bank certificate to this effect and so asked Abbas Salem Al-Shatti to transfer the equivalent of such an amount in Kuwaiti Dinars into his account so he could get a certificate from the bank showing the balance. The money would be given back as soon as the certificate was issued. Mr. Abbas told Srinivas that it would not be a problem and he would speak to his daughter, who was a general manager at one of the leading banks in Kuwait. After speaking to her, he told Srinivas to go to the bank the next morning and meet his daughter and sign the required papers for transferring and retransferring the funds. But he added that all expenses incurred in the process would have to be borne by Srinivas – which Srinivas agreed to. The next day, he met Ms. Al-Shatti at her office in the bank. Ms. Al-Shatti arranged for one of her secretaries to take Srinivas to the relevant department and do whatever was necessary. A few papers were signed, the equivalent of a few thousand rupees were paid in KDs as charges and a certificate showing that he had a bank balance of about fifty lakhs (Indian Rupees) was issued to Srinivas. Srinivas profusely thanked the Al-Shattis and told his son to proceed.

As some great thinker said, "Life is governed by a multitude of forces some of which are stranger than fiction." A few weeks ago, Srinivas had been desperate, having no money and low morale. All it took was one such coincidence to convince him that the Almighty is there, up above the clouds, with a design to protect him. Srinivas' son obtained the visa, proceeded as planned and went to do his course at Hartford University. Srinivas was able to take care of his education financially.

His next obligation was the completion of his house back home. It took some months for him to attend to that, as his priority had been his son's education. Once that was settled, he turned his attentions to the completion of the house. By that time, some of his wife's brothers, pretending to feel bad that the house was not completed, said they would like to help. One of them asked why a piece of land, two and a half acres in size, lying at the tip of her areca plantation, was being left uncultivated. His son expressed a desire to take it over and plant areca in that area. "Just sell that to him, take the money and complete your house," the brother said.

Srinivas' wife was quite intelligent, but her view and thinking extended only to the boundary of her premises, to the village and its surroundings. Though she had lived about twenty years in Kuwait with Srinivas, her mindset was still narrow, feudalistic like that of her brothers'. It was firmly ingrained in them due to the way they had been raised. Pretentions and opportunistic love were common between them, but sincerity and honesty in approach was rare. This seemingly genuine concern of her brother made her sell the land to him at a throwaway price, one much lower than the market price. To help his sister, the brother said, he would ask his son to supervise the construction. He said she could pay him whatever she wanted as a fee. All this sympathy poured in only because the brother had his eye on the fertile land adjacent to their plot.

Srinivas was not informed of this development initially. Only after the first payment of money had been made, to start the remaining work, did he learn of it. Then he was informed that the work was being supervised by her brother's son. He continued sending money until the work was completed and the family shifted from the old house to the newly built one.

In the meantime, several things had happened in Kuwait. The "Souk Al Manaak Crash" – the stock market crash – was one of them. Some prominent families artificially inflated the stock market for some time.

Many people who had been insignificant in the market earlier became millionaires in a short time by investing in shares – even borrowing from banks to finance their investments. Suddenly, the prominent players let the value of their shares come down to their actual levels, which resulted in the busting of the bubble and share prices plummeting. This made some newcomers to the market lose considerably – to the extent, in fact, that they were no more able to maintain their lifestyles and clear their debts. Some went bankrupt. A few committed suicide.

Mr. Al-Hogal, Srinivas' boss, was not an active player in the stock market and didn't lose much. But he bought a commercial complex with a few millions of Kuwaiti Dinars from a member of the royal family. But when he went to occupy it, the caretaker's office told him that it had been purchased by somebody else as per their records, and that he could not occupy it. This was a big shock to him. He went to see the person who had sold it to him, but the person was not available. He was going around visiting Switzerland, London, Las Vegas and other such places and seldom comes home. Mr. Al-Hogal filed a case, produced evidence of his purchase and of transferring money from his account. The case went on for years. Finally, the verdict came in his favor. Then it went to a higher court. After a couple of years, he got the lower court's verdict confirmed by the higher court also. But there was no way to enforce it because there was no asset registered in the seller's name in that area. This process had weakened Al-Hogal financially. He had to sell his travel business, and still found it hard to pay his staff and to carry out his other activities. All the staff knew he would pay them as soon as he got his money back through litigation, but nobody knew when that would be.

From his second year on, Srinivas' son got some financial assistance from the college by teaching students of the lower classes and was almost self-sufficient. He needed money only once in a while. This was a big relief for Srinivas. His residence permit in Kuwait was about to expire and it had become difficult for him to get it renewed as he was nearing sixty, which was the age beyond which foreign nationals were not allowed to work in Kuwait. Though Al-Hogal said he could use his influence to get it renewed for a year or two, Srinivas was not keen and said he would prefer to leave. He had been there five years by now. Though he knew that Al-Hogal would not be able to give him what remained of his salary or any other benefits at the time of his leaving, or even later on for that matter, he decided to go back home, with nothing much to take back.

On completion of his MS degree, Srinivas' son took up employment in the USA itself. Shortly afterwards, he joined up for an MBA course with Kennesaw State University. His eldest brother, Srinivas' eldest son, was working in Bangalore, after doing his MBA, with one of the leading IT firms. He had gotten married to a colleague and settled in Bangalore. Srinivas' two daughters had also married, after completing their degree courses in Bangalore. They had married into good families from Srinivas' native place. The elder daughter was currently living in New Delhi with her husband and the younger one, in the UAE.

Srinivas wound up his residence in Bangalore and returned to his native place, to his newly built house on the property of his wife. She took over the management of the plantation which had, until then, been looked after by one of her brothers. Since his wife was more proficient when it came to supervising agricultural work, Srinivas was more or less free of any really hectic work.

BUSINESS ENCOUNTER AGAIN IN INDIA

Srinivas came across a write-up about a Coimbatore-based company that specialized in the supply and installation of wind, solar and hybrid electricity generating system which could produce electricity in smaller capacities; small enough to be suitable for homes, shops, hospitals, hotels, resorts, schools and colleges. He felt it was a new concept in that area and the business potential would be immense. He wanted to have a tie-up with the company and to represent it for a couple of districts in northern Kerala. He contacted the management of the company who said it would not be a problem, but also said they would need to take a security deposit of a few lakhs of rupees. It was a lean time for Srinivas financially and he decided to enlist a couple of partners and establish a new company to undertake this operation. He found two like-minded partners, retired government officials who were willing to participate, and together they formed a partnership firm with the required capital. They visited the company in Coimbatore had a discussion with them and asked to be shown some installations they had made. There was one wind turbine unit on top of their office itself. Other installations were deep inside Tamil Nadu they said.

The management suggested that, instead of going there, they would show the partners some installations in Kochi and a few nearby places instead. A time to visit these was fixed. An agreement to represent the company was made and the required security deposit was paid against a signed receipt by one of the directors of the company, International Consultancy & Management Services or ICMS. Subsequently, the next week, they all went to Kochi. The company official took them around and showed them one unit in Tagore Park and another at a beach resort on the outskirts of the city.

The team started actively promoting the system. They approached a few customers. The first one was a seaside resort complex comprising of rooms, villas, restaurants, a yoga centre, meditation facilities and so on. It was just starting up its operations. They had a few solar panels, but those were more of an experiment. The management said that they would like to extend the system, and also install wind-generators, to cover the entire complex. Srinivas and his partners contacted the company who said two directors, experts in their field, would visit the next day to assess the availability of wind and prepare an offer. They came the next day as promised. Their names were Mr. Biju Nair and Mrs. Sarita Nair. They were taken to the site. The general manager of the resort showed them around so that the site for the installation of the turbines and additional solar panels could be chosen. Biju Nair measured the wind velocities at different places, zeroed in on a spot, calculated the total energy requirement for the resort and began preparing the offer. Mrs. Sarita Nair prepared the offer while

Mr. Biju dictated it. They offered a system, wind and solar combined, on a turnkey basis and costing about eighteen lakhs. They said that, normally, they would take the full amount in advance, but, in this case, they would be willing to take only 50 percent as their advance. Both Sarita and Biju presented themselves and spoke in such an impressive and knowledgeable way that Srinivas, his partners and the resort's management thought it their good luck that they got in touch with such an expert company. The resort's management agreed to the offer. Since their accountant had gone to another unit belonging to them and was expected to come back only later that day, they said they could either wait or a cheque would be sent later to their office. Quietly, without Biju and Sarita knowing, Srinivas separately asked the management not to cut the cheque in the name of ICMS, but in their company's name. He and his partners took Biju and Sarita to their office and then for lunch at one of the best hotels in the area, assuring them the cheque would be sent to them by courier the next day. They, in turn, said they would send the material along with two workers within the next two days, for building the foundation for the erection of the pole for installing wind turbine. Pole-foundation, they said, might require a few days of curing and only then could they proceed with the installation. Before that, the resort would have to pay the entire amount, since they needed to buy the turbine, controls, wires, storage batteries and so on for the installation of the system.

Mrs. Sarita was pregnant at that time so Srinivas and his partners decided to give her some gift, some item that was a specialty in the area.

Business encounter again in india

Two days later, Biju Nair phoned and said the workers who would be building the foundation for the poles were coming, along with his secretary. They also asked for the payment to be made in cash as some bank holidays were coming up and cashing a cheque might take time.

That morning, a local paper reported that a business couple by the name of Mr. Biju Nair and Mrs. Sarita Nair had been arrested by the Coimbatore Crime Branch for swindling crores of rupees after promising to install wind and solar power units in some mills in Dindigal and Ooty in Tamil Nadu. Srinivas and his partners were about to take their cash when they saw this report. The secretary of Biju Nair's company was on his way and called to say that he would reach the office in about three hours. Srinivas and his partners didn't tell him that they knew about the arrest of the couple and said they would be waiting for him. Their plan was to hold him there and make him call his office and tell them to come with the security deposit they had received from Srinivas and his partners. The man went on calling to tell them where he was and to make sure that they were waiting with the cash. But the calls stopped after some time. Perhaps he had come across the same bit of news somewhere. Srinivas and his partners tried to contact him, but his phone was switched off. They immediately told the resort about the situation and told them that the money they paid would be returned to them in a few hours.

Biju and Sarita were released on bail, but they were brought to Kerala where case after case had piled up against them. Srinivas and his partners were the only party who had a case in northern Kerala. The police brought them there three or four times and then, through their lawyer, they asked Srinivas and his partners to withdraw the case as they were ready to settle the amount out of court. Srinivas and his partners had asked for a premium as it had been over a year since they'd paid the amount. They had also carried out a lot of promotional work on behalf of ICMS, spending their company's money for ICMS's sake. But their lawyer said that they were not settling any other client as they had a soft corner and a measure of respect for the partners, who were senior citizens.

The partnership firm was wound up.

What next? That was the big question for Srinivas.

ON THE PERSONAL FRONT

"The trajectories of some people's lives are sometimes strange," writes Ravishankar (TNIE).

Srinivas wanted to pause for some time and take stock of his life so far, to look back and see what he had achieved, and to look forward and think about what could lie ahead.

He had nothing remarkable to recall from his childhood. His father, a school teacher hadn't left much wealth by way of money or property, but had taught them certain values which Srinivas would carry all his life: character, honesty, compassion to fellow human beings, a mind to see and listen to the sufferings of unfortunate brethren, a thirst for knowledge and a desire to use it for the improvement of one's life. Coupled with these, some of the hard knocks that Srinivas had faced in life, all the disappointments and suffering he'd endured, had definitely shaped his character too.

In the early days, when he had first started earning, Srinivas had no aim other than helping his family – his three brothers, three sisters, parents and grandmother. Of course, his father had retired and was getting a pension, but Srinivas didn't know how much it was. His elder brother was a government employee and was earning too, but he had a wife, three daughters and a son. The children were all young and, as they grew, they knew that the elder brother, Ramdas, was providing them whatever they want – they never felt deprived of something which other children of their age had. But they never grasped, or were simply not old enough to understand, that it was Srinivas' efforts and earnings behind it. They all grew up, got educated, married and settled down with good partners. Ramdas was a star to his siblings, to all of them except Srijay, who was just younger than Srinivas. Srijay was old enough to understand who was behind Ramdas' apparent success. The two had no love lost between them. Also, the elders knew the facts. But since Ramdas was the only one around, they pretended that Ramdas was responsible for everything they had. Ramdas bought some properties and registered them in their mother's name. These were reregistered in his name just before their mother died. Though he was unkind and ungracious to Srinivas, he was a little scared of Srijay for his frank manner and sharp tongue. Ramdas was quite popular with the public and revered by local intellects as he was usually an invitee and active participant at all the functions and festivals in the area. Perhaps, as Senior Superintendent of Post offices, the job he retired from, had given him opportunities to travel to most of the villages of northern Kerala which had post offices, for inspection, and interact with the prominent personalities of the area, and this had led to his being given that kind of respect by people. Moreover, he was a convincing conversationalist and writer, an art he had cultivated from his college days.

For whatever reason, Ramdas found a girl for Srinivas to marry, the family was well-known in the community and were large landholders. She had studied up to the secondary level and was helping with household activities then. After marriage, she was reluctant to leave her village and go with Srinivas to Kuwait, but her brothers were keen to see her off. Srinivas still wondered whether it was due to their desire to see their sister with her husband, or at the thought that they could enjoy the income from her share of property by themselves. They were six brothers and only one sister. Some of the brothers were very broad-minded and loving, but a couple of them were selfish, jealous and very short-sighted. During the first communist ministry in Kerala, led by E. M. S. Namboodiripad, the Land-Reform Act was introduced and they'd had to relinquish their holdings with the tenants. Besides, as per the act, they could only keep sixteen acres for each adult member in the family, and the rest was to be surrendered to the government as excess land, for distribution among landless peasants.

Srinivas had great expectations for his wife, like any young man of his age and background would. He wanted her to be loving, understanding, cultured and compassionate. But he found his wife to be just opposite of all those qualities. There was one particular incident Srinivas always recalled as a sign of how things were going to be in the future.

Before marriage, Srinivas had been living in a lodge with some others. Among them were a few good friends of his. When he got married and brought his wife there, they had come to see and congratulate the couple with some small gift. She was in the bedroom. Srinivas told her to prepare some tea and come out and say hello to them, maybe say a couple of words if she liked. She refused to come to the sitting room, saying she didn't want to see unknown people.

The friends had to leave without seeing her even. Srinivas felt very bad about it. She displayed this kind of arrogance throughout their marriage. She never bothered about what others thought of her words or actions. To Srinivas, she talked in a very arrogant and boisterous way.

Two of their children were born within about three years of the marriage and she was totally at a loss when it came to caring for them in a loving, motherly way. She considered the children's waking up and crying during the nights a nuisance. It was Srinivas who attended to the children in their early years. After the other two children were born, in the next five to six years, it became too much for her to take care of all four in a foreign land where there were no relatives or close neighbors. They decided to put two of the children in a boarding school near their hometown and asked some close relatives who lived nearby to visit them frequently and take them to their home during shorter holidays. Srinivas used to bring them to Kuwait during their long holidays. After the children had spent about four or five years in boarding school, they were brought back to Kuwait and enrolled in a school there. The wife's irrational and crude behavior towards Srinivas and the children continued. Srinivas was afraid that his children might learn this type of behavior. But, thankfully, most of the time, the children were at school, or studying, or watching television, or playing. So they rarely got the time to be exposed to her idiosyncratic behavior at home.

However, Srinivas felt that they should learn some order and discipline, apart from cultivating good manners and becoming confident in life. So he decided to put them in a

On the personal front

good boarding school. But his wife insisted that the youngest son and daughter should stay with them. So Srinivas put the two older children in a reputed residential school near Ooty, in Tamil Nadu. They studied there until the eldest child, their oldest daughter, completed her tenth standard.

This was around the time when Srinivas had left the cable company and settled in Bangalore. He enrolled his three younger children at Bishop Cotton Boys and Girls School and the eldest one in Jyothi Nivas College.

The children completed their education. The daughters got married and were with their respective husbands in New Delhi and the UAE. His eldest son was working with a leading IT company in Bangalore, had married a colleague of his and settled in Bangalore itself. The youngest one, after completing his MS and MBA in the US, got married to a girl chosen by his parents, who too had completed her MS from Texas University and was planning to find employment in the US. With the children settled in different places, Srinivas and his wife decided to leave Bangalore and move back to their native village. With enough income coming in from her property, and nothing much from Srinivas, the arrogance of his wife increased exponentially. Her behavior towards him became ever more hostile, arrogant and hubristic; it was as if she was acting with a vengeance. In the midst of one of their bickering sessions, she told him she would have been much happier if she had married the man she had liked in her school-days and lived with him in the village instead of marrying Srinivas and going to Kuwait. This was new information to Srinivas and he asked her who the man was. She said it was a teacher who used to take tuition classes for her when she had been in school. Apparently they had liked each other. Srinivas asked her why they haven't got married then. She told him the man was not from a family that could match hers and she had been afraid to tell her parents or brothers who, with their feudalistic mindset in those days, might have even caused danger to his life. Srinivas thought that this adolescent incident might still be in her subconscious mind and that she might have been taking him as the villain who had come in between her and her love. He imagined that could be the reason for her hostile and vengeful behavior towards him.

There was also an unfortunate incident which became a reason for her to squabble continuously with him. One of her "loving" brothers – who was known to be a specialist when it came to encouraging fights by adding fuel to the fire – did his best to see that the rift between husband and wife persisted. This brother would constantly counsel his sister, to the point where he had almost complete control over her. And he used to give malicious advice to her so as to ensure, for whatever reasons, that Srinivas never had any say in matters relating to her property.

THE TALE OF RICHARD'S FAMILY

During his days in the granite business, Srinivas had an associate, an elderly man named Richard who had a lot of knowledge about the area, quarries, the different type of granite, the government procedures involved, buyers and so on. His family consisted of wife, two sons and two daughters. One son worked for the Karnataka Government and the other one worked in Saudi Arabia. They had married early and had school-going children by the time Srinivas got to know them. Richard was struggling to get his two daughters married. The girls were good-looking and educated. One was a graduate and the other a B. Ed teacher. But Richard did not have the means to provide large dowries or other perks to a prospective groom unfortunately. His sons wanted to help out, but their wives would not let them meet or do any favors for the sisters or parents. They were originally from Tamil Nadu and had settled in Karnataka.

Somehow, Richard got his elder daughter married to a doctor working in Vellore Hospital. It was his second marriage. His first wife had died and he had two small children. And he wanted a wife to look after him and the kids. After a couple of years, he had another daughter with his new wife. As the children grew, there used to be some quarrels at home between the children for some minor reasons, which invariably spread to the couple. But as the days passed, the fights became routine. Finally, after about fourteen years of marriage, the doctor left his wife and daughter at her parent's house. He then cut all communication with them. He would not call or return their calls or reply to their letters, or even meet them if they went there. The elder daughter was compelled to look for a job and finally got one as a salesgirl in Bangalore. So Richard and his family moved to Bangalore from their village and were staying in a rented house in a housing colony. The youngest daughter of Richard was working at a well-known public school in Bangalore. She used to come from her village and return after school, every day. Shifting to Bangalore was a relief for her as well.

Richard, his wife, his two daughters and granddaughter made up the family. Their main income was the rent they received from their house back in the village, a few hundreds of rupees, along with the salary of the sales girl and the teacher. Richard also made some money as a consultant in the granite field. It wasn't much, but they were happy with it.

Most weekends, the eldest daughter and her child used to go to Vellore. But the doctor and his children, upon seeing them, would go out and not return until the night. The eldest daughter would wait for him there, for some hours, and come back before the night. She insisted that the doctor still loved her and that it was his daughters who did not allow him to meet, talk to or accept her. She hoped that one day, when the daughters were married and gone and he was alone, he would take her and their daughter back.

The tale of richard's family

The little girl was brilliant and they were sending her to a nearby government school. Richard's wife was not in good health and was on medication. A good chunk of the family's income was used to pay for medicines and hospital visits.

Srinivas used to visit them, especially when he needed the services of Richard. Mobile phones had still not really caught on in those days and Richard had no landline at home either. So Srinivas had no choice but to go there in case he wanted to contact him.

One day, Srinivas heard that Richard had died of a heart attack. His photo was printed in the local newspaper as he was quite popular. He had been hospitalized for a couple of days before his death, but Srinivas hadn't known that. He wondered if one of Richard's sons or somebody else had come to help the family since it was only four women left now. Three months after Richard died, it was an Easter Sunday and Srinivas decided to go to see them. When he got there, he found the door open and heard somebody inside shouting at the top of his voice, asking the inhabitants to leave the house with their belongings. Srinivas knew they were a decent family; the girls were quite humble, subdued and of good character. He asked the man who was shouting what the matter was. He hurled a few abuses at the family and said that the rent had not been paid for the last two months. He was the local pawnbroker and the owner of the house. The girls were crying and stammered and sobbed that they had borrowed money to pay the hospital bills and for the last rites of their father. They had to clear the debt and so couldn't pay the rent. But they promised to pay next month. But the owner was not prepared to listen and said he would throw them and their possessions out if they did not move right then. Their helplessness touched Srinivas. He had come across people in such helpless situations many a time in his childhood. He checked and found that he had some money with him. He gave this to the owner and told him that he could collect the balance of that month's rent the next day. He added that the family could only move out at the end of the month, since they had to first find another house. The owner agreed.

Srinivas then told the family to find alternative accommodation as soon as possible and leave that place. The search for a new house continued for days. The family found a few good flats and houses at reasonable rates which they could afford. But as soon as the owners learnt that four females were coming to stay, they started making excuses and denied them the house. This happened several times. Srinivas went to check on the family three days before the end of the month to see when they would be vacating. They were in tears as they explained the situation. He accompanied them to see some of the owners again they had met earlier and spoke on their behalf, but he found the owners were quite adamant. He returned home then, asking the family to try their best again.

He considered various possibilities when he got home. He remembered that he had recently bought a flat for his brother Kiran, whom he had once brought to Mumbai to train at Airworks for three years as an unpaid apprentice, and then also taken to Kuwait and fixed up as an instrumentation engineer for a government ministry. The builder of the flats was a friend of Srinivas, and he had got

The tale of richard's family

a special price for the flat. Presently, the flat was locked and nobody was staying there. Srinivas decided that if the worst came to pass, he would accommodate the family of Richard there until they found another place.

The final day came and, as Srinivas expected, the family was not able to find another house or flat. They begged the owner for more time, but he refused to let them stay there any longer. Perhaps he had found someone who was willing to pay a higher rent. Srinivas told them about Kiran's flat and said that they could stay there until an alternative was found. They moved in there, and stayed for about ten months. Then Kiran said that he and his family were coming on leave and that they would need the flat to be vacated.

All the while the family stayed there, Srinivas visited them whenever he found the time, to ensure the flat was not being spoiled or misused. He was impressed by the polite and loving behavior of the family, especially the younger daughter, the teacher. His own home was a constant storm of nagging by his wife. Sometimes her nagging even turned into abuse and insults. He escaped it whenever it became intolerable and found solace in the company of Richard's family, especially the teacher. Slowly, he became intimate with her. He was a family man with grown up children and he knew such a relation with a lady in her mid-thirties was wrong, but he did not feel guilty as he had never received the love and understanding of a woman. In front of relatives and visitors she pretended to be the ideal wife, but, in truth, she seemed intent on making his life miserable. The love, kindness, affection and understanding of a woman were almost novel to Srinivas and he got it in plenty from this lady, and he never felt at all guilty about the relationship. After a few months, just before Kiran and his family arrived, the family of Richard found a house through a relative of theirs, in a village about thirty kilometers from the city, and moved. Richard's wife paid a nominal rent to Kiran's wife for the period they stayed there. After moving out from the city, the frequency of Srinivas' visits reduced though he still helped them when they needed it. But after a while, he kept away from them totally because his financial condition had become so bad that he could not help them anymore. His relationship with the teacher had started out of compassion for her and pity for her family's sufferings, but now he realized he was not in a position to help anybody. And compassion without being able to succor is the worst thing, capable of creating a truly miserable situation. So Srinivas decided to keep away and leave them to their fate. He never met or even contacted any of them again. Eventually, he left for Kuwait once more.

Then, Srinivas made the greatest blunder of his life. During one particularly bad fight with his wife, he told her about Richard's family and said he had found all the qualities of an ideal woman in the teacher. He said that it was only through them that he understood how graceful a woman could really be. This caused her to explode and she started telling everybody she met about the matter. She told friends, relatives and even workers and the children, adding some of her own additions to the story. And her brother, the one who had a talent for making a bad situation worse, used it as a tool to make her angry again, whenever he felt she was calming down.

SRINIVAS IN THE NORTH EAST

Srinivas felt miserable at home, humiliated by the continuous nagging of his wife. He decided to go somewhere far away and doing something there. He had the address of a wind-solar system supplying company near Coimbatore. Not ICMS, but another one. He decided to verify how genuine this company was. He found that it was a young and reliable company, busy with orders and installation work. In just two years or so, after first starting operations out of a small room in an old industrial shed, they had bought two acres of industrial land and were in the process of building a corporate office, a workshop, a spare parts store and a yard. Srinivas contacted his former partners and asked whether they would be willing to try another venture, this time with a reliable company. They told him that going again to the same customers under another banner and with a new story would be too tiresome and declined. Then Srinivas went back to his earlier idea of going to some place far away and trying his luck. He decided to go to the North East region of India. In the meantime, he also executed an agreement with the wind-solar system supplying company, Windcare India Pvt Ltd. He offered to be their sole representative for the entire Northeast region. He headed for Meghalaya.

Meghalaya, literally the "Abode of Clouds," is a small state that had been carved out of Assam. It has a total land area of 22,429 kilometers. The terrain is made of hills, narrow vales, lakes, hot springs, caves and numerous small streams, all arranged in such a way that it seemed as if the Creator, the Almighty, became confused while assembling these and just thrown in a hap-hazard way in the region. Lying at an altitude of 1496 meters above sea level, the state is also called "The Scotland of the East." It is bound to the north and the east by the state of Assam and to the south and the west by Bangladesh.

Srinivas had to start somewhere. Given his limited financial resources, he tried to look for a decent but economical place to stay. Finally, he decided to stay at the Youth Hostel in Shillong for a while and tried to recall the names of some people he might know there. He sat and thought for some time, and suddenly remembered Mr. P. A. Sangma, a politician and former speaker in the Lok Sabha and a former union minister. Srinivas landed in Shillong, the capital of Meghalaya, and Mr. Sangma was in Tura, which was over three hundred kilometers from there and served as the district headquarters for West Garo Hills. Now Srinivas had to find some way to approach Mr. Sangma. He phoned an advocate friend of his who was an upcoming politician and a disciple of Mr. Oscar Fernandez, in Bangalore. Srinivas used to go to Mr. Fernandez's house sometimes with this advocate friend. He imagined the man might remember him if his advocate friend explained to him. He told his friend that he was in Meghalaya on a business mission and that he would like to meet Mr. sangma to discuss business.

Srinivas asked whether it would be possible for him to tell Mr. Fernandez to phone Mr. Sangma and request him to extend his cooperation. The friend said he would talk to his mentor.

Srinivas fixed up a date and time to meet with Mr. Sangma. He went to Tura, to their house. Mr. Sangma, along with son Conrad Sangma (who was a MLA and had been a minister in the Meghalaya Assembly when his brother was the chief minister) met Srinivas. Srinivas told them about wind-solar electricity generating systems and his intention to market these in Meghalaya and other neighboring states. They were enthused by the idea because there were several areas in the state where there was no electricity. This system, they knew, could be very useful. They asked if any major installation had been done in Meghalaya already, to which Srinivas replied that he had arrived there only about a week ago. Mr. Sangma introduced him to the director of the Meghalaya Non-conventional & Alternate Energy Development Authority (MNREDA) and to the undersecretary of the Ministry of Power. Mr. Conrad, his son, said he would be in Shillong the next week as the assembly would be in session and that Srinivas could meet him there to discuss the matter further. Several phone calls were made and received during the course of the meeting and, from the bits and pieces he heard of their conversations, Srinivas felt that their mind was not in alternate energy system, but were in planning an alternate government, toppling the present one. They asked Srinivas to be in touch, told him not to hesitate to contact them in case he needed help, exchanged all the usual courtesies before saying goodbye.

Srinivas met the director of the MNREDA, Mr. John Rodborne. He said they were going to conduct a seminar on alternate energy and had a very intensive program for implementing alternate energy projects in different parts of the state. He said Srinivas should wait for the announcements. Next, Srinivas met the undersecretary of the Ministry of Power. He told Srinivas to meet Mr. R. G. Lingdoh, the Chairman of Meghalaya Rural Development Corporation, (MRDC) a public-private venture. Mr. Lingdoh was a former interior minister of Meghalaya. Mr. Daniel Ingty, an IAS officer deputed by the Ministry of Power, was the project director. The aim of the corporation was overall development of the rural areas in Meghalaya: in providing housing, education, electrification of the area, skill-development and so on. Mr. Ingty explained the program in detail to Srinivas and said he could give Windcare ten clusters, each cluster of villages consisting of 200 families, initially for community electrification and street-lighting systems. He added that Windcare would have to work on a partnership basis. This meant that out of each progress payment they got for their services, about 30 percent would be retained by the MRDC. On completion, he said, Windcare could take up another ten clusters. This partnership or retention was to ensure that the job was not left in the middle without completion.

Apart from the MRDC, some private enterprises too were interested in having wind-solar hybrid systems of different capacities, and they were ready to pay an advance of up to 50 percent of the project cost. Srinivas, due to his earlier experience with ICMS, was reluctant to accept any advance money. He asked Windcare to visit Shillong as soon as possible, but the company went on postponing the visit.

In the meantime, Srinivas visited Arunachal Pradesh and met the director of the Arunachal Pradesh Energy Development Agency (APEDA), Mr. Marki Loya, in Itanagar. He was very happy because they were just about to start a "Border Area Illumination Program" on the border with China and only one company had come forward to quote so far. He was looking for more companies and so gladly welcomed Windcare. He said he would send one of his officers, someone familiar with wind-mapping at the border area, and that Windcare could immediately proceed and give them a proposal for whatever extent of the total area they could electrify by Wind/Solar system. He said that once the company was on the job, there would be enough work to continue for a long time

Srinivas went to the Windcare office in Coimbatore and discussed the potential of the North East. But they said they were busy with projects in Coimbatore and nearby areas because a lot of major wind electricity generators had been set up in the area recently and Windcare had almost achieved a monopoly in signing the Annual Maintenance Contracts with these. The government of India was providing a tax exemption for the amount invested in wind energy projects, and many companies which were making large profits were investing in WEGs to save tax. A remarkable advantage was that the gestation period was comparatively very short. In about six months, a unit could be ready and the income could start via sale of the electricity to the main grid of the Electricity Board. Such an attractive proposal made many large companies to set up large scale, megawatt scale, units in that area. And Windcare had established themselves as a reliable service-cum-maintenance company and were quite busy. So they naturally didn't show much interest in taking up jobs in the trouble-prone North East.

Srinivas found the Coimbatore-based company was not showing much interest in long-term work or entering into an agreement with MRDA. And he was not prepared to take any advance for selling smaller units or systems as the customers were all influential people and in case the Coimbatore company failed to execute a project as agreed, they could make Srinivas' life miserable. That was why Srinivas had wanted the official from Windcare to come down, discuss and undertake the orders themselves. By now, Srinivas' financial situation was becoming dire. One day, he walked to one of the leading convent schools nearby and explained his educational and work background to the principal, a priest, and told him that he was looking for a job as teacher. The principal thought for a while and then phoned up Dr. Verghese, who was the director of a chain of residential schools in Meghalaya, Assam and Manipur. After their discussion, the father told Srinivas to meet Dr. Verghese the next morning and gave him the address and told him how to reach his office. The next morning, after a short discussion, Dr. Verghese asked Srinivas to join one of his residential schools at Umiam, about forty kilometers from Shillong. Besides boarding and lodging, he was offered a reasonably good salary as well.

Srinivas was taken to the School at Umiam in the Barapani area. He met the chief there, got his accommodation and started work the next day. It was class IV to X that he had to teach English to. He enjoyed the job, and except for a few naughty boys and girls, the rest were very warm and they liked each other. During the weekends, mostly Saturdays, he used to go to meet his friends in Shillong and the neighboring areas. He completed one full academic year there and then decided to quit since he felt a sort of tied-down. He was the kind who liked to be able to move as and when he wanted. He resigned from the school. By that time, there was a strong bond between him and some of his students and colleagues. His leaving there caused some sadness. He went back to the hostel at Lachumiere.

By the time he took up the teacher's job, he had visited most of the important places in Meghalaya like Chirapunji, some famous caves and parks, Tura, Williamnagar, suburbs of Shillong like Balpakram, Rongra, Jakrem, Nongstoin, Nongpoh, Shillong Peak, Nongthymai, Mawphlang and so on. And also Naharlagun and Itanagar in Arunachal Pradesh, Gauhati, Dispur, Jorhat, Kaziranga and Rangapara in Assam.

Srinivas decided to go back to pursuing his favorite line: business. But he knew also that unless he had strong technical, organizational and financial support from some established company, he could not afford to proceed further. Windcare might provide technical support, yes. But financially? Srinivas spoke with a couple of local companies with which he'd had some interactions earlier. One was Eco Consultants, owned by Mr. Nabha Bhatacharjee and his Meghalayan wife. The other was Power Carriers India Pvt Ltd. whose chairman was Mr. Wallamphong Roy and one of the directors was Mr. Pradip Pillai. The former was closely working with the MNREDA. He had supplied and installed some WEGs. The latter was working as a contractor to the Ministry of Power, supplying and installing electricity distribution systems. Nabha showed some interest in a cooperation arrangement. He asked Srinivas to use his office for any business matter, and promised to find suitable accommodation for him. He collected information about the contacts made by Srinivas, their potential, and the progress he had made on these. Also, at his request, Srinivas introduced him to a prominent consultant and contracting company in Delhi, owned by a technocrat returned from America. He was an expert on alternate energy systems, mainly wind and solar, and Srinivas had a close association with him. Later on, after collecting all information, he started distancing himself from Srinivas. When Srinivas tried reaching him, he was always not available or busy. Srinivas understood his game and just ignored it.

He spoke then with Power Carriers who, he felt, were more honest and sincere. Mr. Wallamphong Roy and Mr. Pillai said they wanted to go in for diversification and that this line of business was quite appealing to them. They, at present, were flooded with contracts from the ministry for their primary field. But the payment for several jobs they had executed were yet to be received. And the two men earnestly wanted to diversify into an alternative field. The ministry was financially in bad shape, perhaps due to various subsidies and other freebies the political establishment was offering to increase their vote bank. However, the men at Power Carriers said their annual general body meeting was due in a couple of months. It would be held in Kerala as a couple of directors were from there. They promised that the issue would be taken up during the meeting. Roy confessed though that he didn't know much about the field of wind and solar energy and therefore asked Srinivas to prepare a project report by then, so that he could present it to the company's board for discussion. He offered Srinivas their guesthouse, so that he could stay and work there comfortably.

Srinivas visited some places around the region, collected the necessary data and started working on the project report. It took over a month for him to complete it. The directors, Mr. Wallamphong Roy and Mr. Pillai, were so impressed that they wanted to pay a token fee for his report. Since the final decision on starting a new division in the line of alternate energy field would likely be delayed until the board meeting, Srinivas decided to go back home. He had spent three years in the North East by then. He left for Delhi, where his daughter, son-in-law and their children lived. He stayed there for a few weeks and then left for his native village. He didn't know that a big surprise was waiting for him there.

A FRESH HOPE

Life is a journey. Short and straightforward for some. Long and filled with mountains and valleys for some others. Over the course of the journey, one meets all sorts of people, people of different creeds, temperaments, customs and nature. As time passes, memories of some of them stay with us while others fade away. When Srinivas got back home, he received a mail from a man who remembered him from the time he had been staying in Geneva, while working on his finance project all those years ago. His name was Martin Johnson. Srinivas vaguely remembered having met

A fresh hope

him at one of the offices he used to frequent to collect some documentation.

In his email, Mr. Martin stated that, shortly after they had met, he had left for South America in search of greener pastures. He had made his way through a few countries there and settled in Venezuela, a country rich in oil. He had started, with some contractor, an oil-related business. He had slowly started taking up contracts by himself and soon became a well-known major contractor in the field. In the course of building up a career for himself as a contractor and accumulating money, he said, he had become so caught up in his work that he had not cared to marry and build up a family. Now all that was left in his life was money and a fatal disease, lung cancer, that he had contracted during his oil-field activities, and for which he was presently undergoing treatment.

In his message, he said that he had a fixed deposit of 500 million US dollars with the Hong Kong & Shanghai Banking Corporation (HSBC). He had managed to find the registered address of "Dr.Srinivas & Associates" and an email ID through the Chamber of Commerce. Since he knew Srinivas to be a sincere, trustworthy and honest family man, he said that he would like to do some passive business in India with Srinivas as a partner, once he had recovered sufficiently from his present ailment. He asked Srinivas to suggest a few business ventures they could get into. Srinivas told him about some businesses which could be managed without too much strain, by delegating tasks to competent executives. In such businesses, Mr. Martin could take it easy and manage things with Srinivas' overall assistance.

Srinivas said that, if Martin could travel to India, Srinivas could even arrange for him to be admitted for treatment in one of the best hospitals in Bombay, where medical treatment was considered world-class.

A few days later, Martin Johnson wrote back saying that he'd had another medical check-up and that the diagnosis was that he was suffering from chronic esophageal cancer and needed surgery at the earliest. It was decided that he would have the operation in a hospital in Chile. Since he was afraid that HSBC might cause problems in releasing the deposit in favor of Srinivas, in case something serious happened to him, he wrote at once to HSBC asking them to release the funds in Srinivas' favor, against the furnishing of his passport number, permanent address and bank account to HSBC. He also sent Photostat copies of the FD receipt, a copy of his Swiss passport and the request he'd made to HSBC, (addressed to its chairman) his telephone numbers and the names of the officers in charge of the Asia-Pacific operations of HSBC in Hong Kong (Mrs. Nina Lal Kidwai and Mr. Vincent Cheng). Accordingly, Srinivas contacted HSBC, Hong Kong, who confirmed the deposit and the receipt of the instruction from Mr. Martin Johnson. They asked him to send his passport details, his permanent address and the account to which the amount was to be transferred. These were provided. But then there was no communication from the bank for a while. Upon sending them a couple of reminders, HSBC replied that Martin Johnson was no more and that they had transferred the funds to Bank Rikayet Indonesia (BRI), one of their associate banks, and asked him to contact them. When he contacted them, their director of foreign exchange operations, Dr. Dato Hussein, confirmed the transfer in Srinivas' name, but said that the amount was being kept in a suspense account subject to his satisfying certain formalities. The director said Srinivas had to open an account with their bank immediately, with a minimum deposit of 1000 dollars so that the funds could be transferred from the suspense account to his account. To authenticate his position in the bank, he sent the copy of his identity card as well.

Srinivas decided to go to Djakarta, confirm all the details and only then open the account. When he got there, he went to BRI bank and learned that the bank was a leading one in Indonesia with several branches and ATMs in the city of Djakarta. He contacted the director of the foreign exchange department, met him and opened an account. He was told that the process of opening an account might take some time and that he could go back to the hotel and that the passbook and other documents would be brought to him there in the evening. The director came that evening to the hotel, as promised, and handed over the passbook with a credit balance of 500,001,000 dollars and an ATM card. He told Srinivas that the amount had already been credited to his account. He could withdraw the amount online, but was advised to credit an amount of 400,000 dollars to his account first to make it active as per their central bank's regulations. Srinivas said that would be impossible for him at this juncture. The Director told him that the money would only be going into his account, and that he should try and make arrangements for remitting this amount as foreign exchange regulations stipulated this condition. The next day, Srinivas went back home.

On getting back home, Srinivas informed the director that he was not in a position to make such a remittance. The bank gave him a cut-off date and said that unless he made this payment by then, the entire amount would go to their central bank and would either be confiscated or would be disposed of in a way they deemed fit. Srinivas didn't respond to this. The bank sent him a few reminders and then there was a long silence.

A few months later, Srinivas got a letter, supposedly from the accounts officer, one Mr. Richard Brown, of Ulster Bank in Belfast, Ireland. He wrote on behalf of the bank saying that an amount of 500 million dollars had been transferred to them with Srinivas as the beneficiary. They had also got his address and passport number. Srinivas was provided with his account number at Ulster Bank, and phone-banking details, an ID and a password so he could verify the status of his account at any time. He verified it several times using the password and ID, first alone and then with some of his friends. The bank informed him that he could transfer the amount at anytime to his designated account and sent a form for him to fill, sign and send back. Before the transferring was done, he had to make a payment of about 52,000 dollars as currency fluctuation adjustment charges. Also, they told him that there could be a tax, while transferring, of around 5750 pounds sterling.

Srinivas was totally confused. 500 million dollars! It was the GDP of a small country! And he was going to get it as an inheritance! Could it be true? All the correspondence was under the letterhead and on the documents of Ulster Bank PLC. And he'd also been given the phone-banking details.

A fresh hope

He made it a point to hear the announcement that was made, after he had typed out his ID and password, welcoming him by stating his full name and the amount in his account. He let some of his close associates hear this announcement. But how was he to organize the currency fluctuation difference, tax amount and such now? He thought about it for several days.

He had some money with him, which he had made by selling a small property given to him by the eldest of his three sisters, Nalinii S. Nair, part of the inheritance she got from mother by way of a will, in which this property was exclusively kept for three daughters and Ramdas. Since she knew that Srinivas was not financially sound now, she wanted to give him a portion of this property. She had discussed it with her husband, Mr. S. Nair, a man of principles who had earned a reputation for himself in his department as a corruption-free officer, who readily agreed to her proposal. S. Nair, who had retired as a deputy commissioner of commercial taxes was an honest, straightforward and corruption-free person in a realm where people run after, sometimes even bribing higher officials, to get posted in some jurisdictions, check-posts and so on. He used to request his seniors to help him by *not* get a posting to such places. There were occasions, during some tax-evasion raids led by him on powerful business houses, where his very life was in danger and he escaped only by the grace of divine providence. Srinivas sometimes felt proud that he was his brother-in-low.

His sister had had only one condition when she'd given Srinivas the land – that he shouldn't try and get into any more business ventures now that he was getting older. She told him to deposit the proceeds of the sale in a bank and use the interest he would receive off it to live a peaceful life. Srinivas was hesitant to go against her ruling, but the temptation for bigger money and the thought of the possibilities, especially things he could do a lot of humanitarian projects to help people less fortunate than him and so on, proved irresistible. Srinivas figured that, with so large an amount, he could help many people and spend his twilight years engaged in some humanitarian services. He knew that the money he had in hand now would not be sufficient to meet the conditions of Ulster Bank, but it would help him cover the expenses he would incur on his quest to find enough finance for this project.

Finally, he decided to go to the UAE where he had some businessmen friends and well-wishers. In the UAE, there was a company run by two partners who Srinivas had known for a long time. They were quite sincere, hard-working and successful businessmen. One of the partners was distantly related to him even. Whenever he was in the UAE, he always enjoyed their hospitality. Srinivas told them about the situation. Without any hesitation, they agreed to help him – on condition that he returned their money as soon he got part of the amount or the full amount. They provided certain amount and this coupled with the money Srinivas had in hand was enough to pay the currency fluctuation difference and tax amount. The form for transfer of the amount, sent by Ulster Bank, was filled in and Srinivas asked them to transfer five million dollars initially to a bank in the UAE. The next day, the accounts officer, Richard Brown, confirmed that they would arrange to transfer this amount. Copies of two "tested telex"' messages were then sent from

A fresh hope

Ulster Bank in Belfast, transferring two million and three million dollars through their London headquarters.

Srinivas checked with his bank in the UAE and found that no money had reached his account. He contacted the accounts officer, Brown, who said that the Bank of England, the central bank of the UK, had withheld the transfer because there was a mandatory levy on foreign deposits going out of the country called the "foreign payment beneficiary insurance" – which was one percent of the amount. In this case, it worked out to 50,000 dollars. Ulster Bank gave him a final date before which the payment had to be made, or else the money would go to the Bank of England, the UK's central bank.

Srinivas' suspicions were aroused by these demands coming one after the other. He felt he should investigate a little before he made another payment. He applied for a British visa so that he could go there and verify everything personally. Since he had gone there several times before, he did not submit some details which were apparently only necessary for first-time visitors. His application was rejected for want of more documents. He applied again, this time enclosing all required documents as asked. This time, again, he was denied a visa because the official granting the visa felt that Srinivas might take up employment in the UK! Srinivas was actually amused and wondered if the officer was in his right mind. He had been to the UK at least six times in the past, in his prime, and they'd had no such fears back then. But now, when he was in his mid-seventies, the immigration authorities felt that he might be going to look for a job!

As a next step, Srinivas found the name and address of the chief executive of Ulster Bank and sent him a letter explaining what had happened, told him the whole story. He enclosed copies of the letters exchanged between himself and the bank and requested to be told what exactly the present situation was. For a few weeks, he received no reply. He sent reminders and called a couple of times. Then he finally got a mail from the head of the complaint handling centre stating that there was presently no account in his name with a deposit of 500 million dollars and that the individuals he had mentioned were not in the employment of the bank now.

Srinivas was very disappointed. First it had been HSBC and BRI, and now Ulster. He had spent almost 75,000 dollars so far – his own as well as borrowed money. There were records of every transfer he'd made. He complained to the banking ombudsman in London who said that Ulster Bank had informed them that there was no account with them in the name of Srinivas and, therefore, they could not deal with this problem. They asked him to contact "Action Fraud UK: National Fraud & Crime Reporting Centre." A complaint was registered with this office online, who gave Srinivas a case number. But then there was no response from them after that. Srinivas next contacted the "Cybercrime Investigation Cell" in New Delhi, a division of the CBI, who told him to lodge a complaint with the local police in the area concerned. The local police station told him that they didn't have the infrastructure to deal with an international complaint. But they said they would register the complaint and send it to the crime branch. No meaningful response had come from them either.

A fresh hope

In the meantime, Srinivas came across certain documents which revealed that a Libyan, Fathi Hussein Abu Zouda, had produced an authorization letter, apparently given to him by Martin Johnson, which gave him blanket permission to use and handle Martin's bank accounts and assets. This letter had been signed by Martin and witnessed by two individuals. Another letter written by Martin, presumably from his hospital bed at the Metropolitan Hospital Santiago, confirmed giving him general power of attorney to handle all assets of Martin Johnson. And a third document, a sworn affidavit by Abou Zouda, endorsed by the High court of Hong Kong, Special Administrative Region and its registrar, and witnessed by two lawyers of the Hong Kong High Court, said that he was entitled to draw the amount of 500 million dollars from HSBC.

As recently as November and December 2015, Srinivas had received two letters from one David Lipton, a regional officer, supposedly of the IMF office in London. He had attached his IMF identity card, stating that their records showed that some money was outstanding in favor of Srinivas. He asked Srinivas to fill the form attached to the mail, and send it back to them for further processing. Srinivas was by now tired of this sort of thing and did not bother to reply even.

Srinivas was not sure whether such a deposit even existed at all. If at all the statement and deposit of Martin Johnson were real, it was a possibility that this was some high level manipulation by some senior bank officials and lawyers, perhaps even in collusion with some top government personnel, to scuttle the process of it reaching the real beneficiary as the amount was quite significant. Whatever the truth was, the only thing that resulted out of it for Srinivas was a big loss.

Srinivas came back from the UAE. He was rather restless and knew he had to do something to recover from his losses. He thought of going somewhere for a few days to sit and think coolly. He went to Goa. Near his hotel was a small shop which he would often go to. He would sit there and chat with the owner, Lawrance D'souza, who was a pleasant fellow. One day, he said that he had a license to open a restaurant and that it was his life's ambition to run one in his own place. Srinivas asked why he was not starting it then. The man said he didn't have the money. He added that if somebody helped him by giving him about five lakhs, he could start one in a modest way. Before starting his shop, he had been the general manager of a bar-restaurant for over ten years and was familiar with all the aspects of running such an establishment. Srinivas agreed to give him that much, on a Partnership, but confessed he didn't know anything about running a restaurant. They entered into a partnership agreement and Srinivas gave him some of the money and then went home to arrange for the rest of the amount. His plan was to get into something to keep himself engaged so that he could think of avenues where he could do something more to enhance his earnings in order to cover his losses.

Srinivas had some money in a bank. He withdrew it and sent it to Lawrance. The rest he borrowed from his sister Nalini and a cousin. He then returned to Goa and gave it to Lawrance as agreed. The interior of the shop was

A fresh hope

converted into a restaurant, and it was done in a tastefully admirable way. Lawrance also ordered some equipment for the kitchen, crockery, tables and other furniture, did the plumbing and electrification. When the license was looked at, it was noticed that the same had expired a few years ago. Now they had to get a new license or renew the old one. In case of a renewal, he had to pay the fees for the lapsed period as well. Moreover, the procedure was quite cumbersome and applying for a new license was easier. Fees were nominal, but they had to wait for a long time to complete the procedure. There would be inspections by the departments of water, fire, food, electricity and health. In each case, the inspectors came at their own convenience unless "taken care of properly." Lawrance got tired. Since his shop had closed, his income had also dwindled. Once the interior decoration work was over and the restaurant was ready to open, Srinivas decided to take an apartment and stay there so he could prepare for the opening of the restaurant. Lawrance was an honest person. He thought that he could just renew the license in a day or two and was filled with enthusiasm about opening the restaurant. But when he saw the hurdles, the running around between various offices, he got dispirited. He bought a couple of taxis and started letting them out to some taxi company. Gradually, his interest in the restaurant started waning. His attitude became one of "let it come when it comes," true to the "Suse Gard" way. But for Srinivas the situation was different.

It had been over a year since the agreement was made and they'd started investing. Besides, Srinivas had to pay his rent and other expenses without any significant engagement.

Since he joined up as a member with the Goa Management Association, he went for the activities that were frequently held there and met several people. He gave Lawrance an ultimatum: that unless the license came through and the restaurant opened in a months' time, he would have to return whatever money he had invested. Lawrance managed to return the money on the agreed date. Srinivas wound up his establishment there and came back home.

He was in his late seventies by now. And what to do next was the big question…

EPILOGUE

Srinivas sat down and began a retrospection of his life and an assessment of himself. "Am I a failure?" he wondered. "Have I achieved anything? Do I have enough time left for me to do anything worthwhile?" A volley of questions ran through his mind.

When he had quit his studies and started working, his sole aim had been to see to it that his family was restored to their former glory. He craved for them to become one of the most prominent and respected families in the area. The family consisted of four brothers and three sisters, their parents and grandmother. The grandmother and parents had died well-off and happy.

The eldest brother, Ramdas, was now a respectable citizen in the area, living with his own family made up of his wife, three daughters and a son. His eldest daughter was married to Ramesh, whom Srinivas had sent to work with Abu Ali in Kuwait. Though Ramesh left Abu Ali after a few years later, he still lived in the Gulf. His children were all married and well-off.

Ramdas' second daughter was married to a banker. The third daughter was a teacher who had married an engineer and was living happily. His son was the CEO of the company which had been started by Srinivas years ago and had been

Epilogue

looked after by Ramdas. The company had grown greatly by now, with branches in different places. Ramdas was also the chairman of the trust of a local place of worship. He was a well-respected and satisfied person in all ways.

The second child of their parents was Srinivas. His older daughter, married to an engineer, had two children, Anjali and Anurag, who had been born and schooled in Delhi. Her husband was the regional manager of a South Indian company, representing Lloyds Surveyors. Now he had resigned and had come back to help his father, who was old, and to look after their plantation and other properties. Anjali now is an engineer from Shastra Uiversity in Tamilnadu. Srinivas' second child, the older son, was a senior executive at a well-known global IT company in Bangalore. His wife, a colleague of his, was now a teacher at an international school. They had settled in Bangalore, with their two children. The third child of Srinivas, a daughter, formerly married to a bank executive working in Dubai and now separated after fifteen years of marriage, was a teacher at a school near home. The only daughter the couple had, Meghna, was a brilliant and talented girl, first educated in Dubai and later at Chinmaya Mission Residential School in Coimbatore. Now, after completing her BBA at Alliance Business Academy in Bangalore, she was pursuing her higher studies in Canada. The last of Srinivas' four children, his youngest son, after finishing his MS and MBA in the USA, had settled there with his wife and children.

Srinivas was also happy because his wife was a changed woman now. She no longer nagged him like before, though the maladies injected by her brother still remain infected.

Epilogue

She now behaved like the ideal family lady. He discovered that her "loving brother," the one who used to borrow money from her whenever he wanted and give it back whenever he liked, had recently been asked by her to clear the accounts. He hadn't liked that. When she put pressure on him, he did clear but started abusing her and scowling at her. She understood that the man had only been taking advantage of her dependence on him, and finally understood that it might be better to depend on her own husband and children rather than a pretentious brother.

The third brother, Srijay, had always been a bit rebellious. After coming back from the coffee estate, he had bought an ambulance and attached it to a leading hospital in that area. He had expired a couple of years ago. His children, all of them, were in the Gulf, working.

The fourth brother, Kiran, whom Srinivas had fixed up with the Ministry of Electricity & Water in Kuwait had retired, left Kuwait and settled in Bangalore. One of his sons was the head of the Asia-Pacific operations of a well-known telecommunications company based in Singapore. His other son was an executive with an American consulting firm and lived with his parents in Bangalore.

Nalini, the eldest of the sisters, and her husband, S. Nair, a retired official, were leading a peaceful life. Two of their children were living abroad. One was in New Zealand and another in the UAE both with their husbands and children. The eldest daughter, a doctor, a well-known pediatrician in the area, lives in the hometown with her husband, Arun, who is also a doctor.

Epilogue

The second sister, Padmini. K. Nambiar, with her husband, a retired divisional engineer of Southern Railway, lived in the hometown as well. Their children live in different places: Australia, the UAE and Indonesia.

The third sister, Radha Nayanar, still lived in the original family house with her husband, who had retired from Kuwait Airways. Their eldest daughter Praseetha lives in the USA and the other children lived in the UAE.

All of them were well-off, leading glamorous and hectic lives, and none of them had the time to think about anything unpleasant. Many of the grandchildren of his brothers and sisters had never even met Srinivas. Of course Srinivas could not take all the credit for such prosperity, as other players involved were also quite instrumental. He found satisfaction in the fact that a foundation had been built by him for all his family members, and that it had been successfully utilized by them.

Almost no one remembered anymore how he had transformed them into a renowned, well-educated and reputed clan with good spouses, houses, properties and businesses. Maybe Kiran and Nalini remembered the remittances that used to come regularly from Kuwait during their childhood, but that had been long ago and they were certainly too busy now to have the time to remember such things.

All this reminded Srinivas of a recent incident. A cousin of his, a revolutionary in his youth who had later turned into a quiet and ideal family man, had developed about five acres of land next to a road that had then been servicing only bullock carts, though now there was a state highway running along there. To undertake development of the plot and to meet some requirements of his family, this cousin pledged the land to a bank and took a loan of 5,000 rupees. He was not able to repay the amount on the due date. After the usual notices were sent, the bank put the property up for auction. This was during 1980.

The cousin frantically wrote a letter to Srinivas, asking him to send this amount. He also said that, if Srinivas so desired, the property could be transferred to him. All the cousin wanted was to keep his prestige in the area by avoiding a public auction of his property. Srinivas immediately sent him the amount and said that all he wanted was that his cousin not to be subjected to any humiliation. He said he didn't need that land.

The years passed. The cousin himself was no more now and his children were all grown up, employed, married and settled in different places. The area has developed to such an extent that an acre, which had cost a few hundreds of rupees in the late seventies, when his cousin bought it, was now worth crores. The family decided to sell the land. Several claimants, apart from the wife and children, cropped up then – nephews, siblings and so on. The land was sold for a few crores and everyone pocketed a few lakhs and crores.

And nobody remembered the man who had struggled to develop the land, or the man who had come forward to help him when he'd been on the verge of losing it. They didn't know and didn't have the time to care about such things.

Epilogue

But that was how the world worked. As Hillary Clinton said; "I know what it is to be knocked down, and how to dust yourself and get back, up and to keep fighting for what you believe in. There are issues and obstacles that I have to overcome. My one asset is that I have an idealism that has been tempered by time and experience."

"How relevant those words are in my case," Srinivas thought.

As recently as a couple of weeks ago, a mail had come from his old associate in Kuwait, Najim Abdulla Al Safwan, saying that he had been engaged in his business of project-financing for about seven years now. He now had two partners, old contacts whom Srinivas also knew – Alian Robin Boumier, a French National, and William Sherman, an American. They had some good clients scattered over the world and had their office now at 116, Avenue des Champs-Elysees, 75008 Paris. He invited Srinivas to join the group as they felt he was familiar enough with the relevant process and activities, and that he would be of help to them.

'What a twist of fate! And at this age!' Srinivas thought.

Made in the USA
Monee, IL
22 June 2021